SPURS
On This Day

SPURS
On This Day

History, Facts & Figures from Every Day of the Year

DAVID CLAYTON

SPURS
On This Day
History, Facts & Figures
from Every Day of the Year

All statistics, facts and figures are correct as of 31st January 2013

© David Clayton

David Clayton has asserted his rights in accordance with the Copyright, Designs and Patents Act 1988 to be identified as the author of this work.

Published By:
Pitch Publishing (Brighton) Ltd
A2 Yeoman Gate
Yeoman Way
Durrington
BN13 3QZ

Email: info@pitchpublishing.co.uk
Web: www.pitchpublishing.co.uk

First published 2011
Reprinted 2013, 2015, 2018

A catalogue record for this book is available from the British Library.

ISBN 978-1-9054118-6-3

Typesetting and origination by Pitch Publishing.
Printed and bound in India by Replika Press.

For Michael Russell and his little son
Beau Valentine-Russell – THFC born and bred

ACKNOWLEDGEMENTS

Thanks to Dan Tester, my long-suffering editor, for patience above and beyond the call of duty. Thanks to Will Unwin, without whose help I couldn't have completed this book and to Chris Wildgoose.

Thanks to Pitch Publishing for not hiring a team of hit-men to pay me a visit after numerous deadlines sailed past. Thanks to the guys who have produced Spurs websites and books that I've been able to reference from time to time and I owe the chaps behind these labours of love a huge debt of gratitude, and to my best Spurs mate Michael Russell, and his little son Beau, who could one day play down at the Lane (so long as it's me and not his dad that helps him with his technical skills).

A massive thanks to lifelong Lilywhite Dave Hewitt who spotted a couple of inaccuracies in the first edition that slipped through the net – many thanks Dave for all your help. This second edition is dedicated to you.

Most of all, thanks to my family – Sarah my wife and my beautiful children Harry, Jamie and Chrissie for all the lost hours.

INTRODUCTION

Few would disagree that the football world would be a darker, less colourful place without Tottenham Hotspur. If West Ham United claim to be the 'Academy' of English football, White Hart Lane has to be the School for Performing Arts with such artisans as Glenn Hoddle, Ossie Ardiles, Jimmy Greaves, David Ginola and Gazza – to name but a handful – entertaining the Spurs fans over the past 120 or so years.

It's a fine thing, tradition, and from the 'Push and Run' style of Bill Nicholson's double-winning side of 1961 to the current easy-on-the-eye side of today, Tottenham Hotspur Football Club has always sought to play football the right way and send the supporters away with a smile on their face.

With panache and style also comes pitfalls and Spurs have always had a fragility about them and an unpredictability that makes following the club a rollercoaster ride without a seatbelt. But that's why football loves them.

The first non-league club to win the FA Cup, the first club to achieve the 'impossible' double, and the first English team to win a European trophy – hardly a club that underachieves as certain people might suggest…

Spurs On This Day aims to capture the spirit of this very special football club with at least one entry for every day of the year throughout the club's history – and more for busier times.

There are highs and lows, great days and bad, pleasure and frustration. Would any Spurs fans want things any other way?

David Clayton

SPURS
On This Day

JANUARY

WEDNESDAY 1st JANUARY 1930

Percy Smith is appointed the Tottenham manager, arriving from Bury. He was a forward-thinking man, and quickly changed the club's style of play by encouraging the side to pass and move. Smith took the team to Second Division promotion in 1933, finishing third in the top-flight the following season. He left in 1935 after suffering relegation to the Second Division and became manager at Notts County. Later in his career, Smith would take charge at Bristol Rovers, though his legacy of quick, passing and entertaining football continues at White Hart Lane to this day.

MONDAY 1st JANUARY 1996

Gerry Francis' side beat eventual champions Manchester United 4-1 at White Hart Lane. Goals from future United player Teddy Sheringham, Sol Campbell and a Chris Armstrong brace gave Spurs the three points in front of the Sky cameras. The Red Devils weren't helped by goalkeeper Peter Schmeichel going off injured at half-time, though Spurs were full value for their emphatic win.

TUESDAY 1st JANUARY 2002

Dean Richards scores a goal on 44 minutes to give Spurs a 1-0 win over Blackburn Rovers. The victory moves Glenn Hoddle's side up to seventh in the Premier League.

SATURDAY 2nd JANUARY 1982

A Garth Crooks goal settles an FA Cup third-round tie against Arsenal. It was the start of Spurs' defence of a trophy they had won the previous year. This was only the second north London derby in the FA Cup, and attracted a crowd of 38,421. The victory was made even sweeter by the fact Arsenal's goalkeeper and former Spurs favourite, Pat Jennings, was at fault for the winning goal.

SATURDAY 3rd JANUARY 1970

Spurs are unable to defeat Third Division Bradford City in the FA Cup, despite taking a two-goal lead thanks to strikes from Jimmy Greaves and Roger Morgan. The Yorkshire side rally and manage to pull level to force a replay ten days later. At the second time of asking, Spurs run out 5-0 winners at Valley Parade to progress to the next round.

SUNDAY 4th JANUARY 1987

In the 100th north London league derby it is the Gunners who take the spoils, winning 2-1. Arsenal go two up by half-time, with Mitchell Thomas scoring a consolation goal just before the break. At this point, the Gunners were on an 18-match unbeaten run, but Spurs got their own back at the end of the season by finishing one place higher in the table.

WEDNESDAY 4th JANUARY 2005

Spurs leave Old Trafford with a creditable point following a goalless draw against Manchester United, though it would have been all three points but for an astonishing mistake from the linesman. When Pedro Mendes hit a speculative shot from all of 40 yards out, it seemed goalkeeper Roy Carroll would make an easy catch, but instead he dropped the ball a good two yards over his own goal-line before hastily dragging it back into play. The assistant referee failed to spot that it was a legitimate goal, meaning that Spurs were effectively robbed of two points.

SATURDAY 5th JANUARY 1991

A trip to a stormy Blackpool had all the ingredients for an FA Cup upset, but Paul Stewart's lone strike means that Spurs go into the hat for the next round and it's the start of a thrilling journey. Terry Venables' team go all the way to the final, where they defeat Brian Clough's Nottingham Forest at Wembley.

SATURDAY 6th JANUARY 1923

Spurs move further away from the relegation zone with a 2-0 victory over Middlesbrough at White Hart Lane.

SATURDAY 6th JANUARY 1934

Spurs enjoy their biggest win of the season with a 5-1 victory over Aston Villa at White Hart Lane and move into fourth place in Division One as a result. James McCormick scores an early goal, before Tom Meads hits a wonder strike from 25 yards. George Hunt and Les Howe add two more with Spurs rampant and McCormick grabs a fifth before the visitors grab a late consolation.

WEDNESDAY 6th JANUARY 1943

Terry Venables is born in Dagenham. As a player he made 115 league appearances in Tottenham's midfield. He also featured for the likes of Chelsea and Queens Park Rangers at club level and earned two caps for England. As a manager he was more successful; after three years at Barcelona, where he won La Liga and the Copa del Rey, he came back to Spurs. He will be best remembered for the club's 1991 FA Cup victory at Wembley.

SATURDAY 6th JANUARY 1962

Blizzard-like conditions were a cause for concern for the FA Cup holders as they took on Birmingham City. A pulsating match ended in a 3-3 draw, with Jimmy Greaves scoring either side of a Cliff Jones goal to ensure that Spurs would get a second chance to progress to the next round, which they gladly took, winning 4-2 at White Hart Lane a week later.

SATURDAY 7th JANUARY 1984

A goalless draw against Fulham will always be remembered for defender Graham Roberts being forced to go in goal after keeper Ray Clemence was stretchered off injured. The part-time keeper went on to make some important saves to take the game into a replay. Roberts actually went on to score in the second tie between the two sides.

SATURDAY 7th JANUARY 1995

Spurs take on Conference side Altrincham at White Hart Lane in the FA Cup third round, reviving memories of the club's epic battle in the late 1970s. In 1979, non-league Altrincham held Tottenham to a 1-1 draw before losing the replay 3-0 at Manchester City's Maine Road. This time there is no cup romance as Gerry Francis' men win 3-0 thanks to goals from Teddy Sheringham, Ronny Rosenthal and Stuart Nethercott.

SATURDAY 8th JANUARY 1921

An emphatic 6-2 first-round victory over Bristol Rovers sets Spurs on their way to the FA Cup Final. Six different players go onto the score-sheet for Tottenham as they dominate the match against the Pirates; the likes of Jimmy Seed and Tommy Clay set Spurs on their way before Bert Smith, Fanny Walden, Jimmy Cantrell and Bert Smith confirm an emphatic victory.

MIDFIELDER AND MANAGER TERRY VENABLES WAS BORN IN JANUARY 1943.

SUNDAY 8th JANUARY 1945

Future Tottenham legend Phil Beal is born in Godstone, Surrey. The defender signs straight from school and goes on to play 333 league games for the club in a career that lasts 12 years. He had the tricky task of taking over from the just-retired Danny Blanchflower, but he managed to establish himself in spite of the size of the shoes he was stepping into. During his time with Spurs he earned FA Cup, League Cup and Uefa Cup winners' medals, though he would lead a nomadic existence in the latter stages of his career with spells in America, before his retiring after a spell at Oxford City.

WEDNESDAY 9th JANUARY 1980

Spurs pull Manchester United out of the hat in the third round of the FA Cup and go on to win 1-0 in extra time as Ossie Ardiles scores with almost the last kick of the match. The victory was made even more special by the fact Glenn Hoddle spent a large portion of the match in goal following an injury to Milija Aleksic.

SATURDAY 10th JANUARY 1970

A struggling Spurs earn a vital 2-1 win over Derby County at White Hart Lane. Jimmy Greaves scores his final league goal for the club, with Roger Morgan claiming the other. Spurs had endured a torrid spell, winning only one game in 11 matches from November onwards.

SATURDAY 11th JANUARY 1975

Spurs' battle against relegation receives a massive boost following a 5-2 win away at Newcastle United. Alfie Conn inspires the side to victory as he nets a hat-trick, with Cyril Knowles and John Duncan also finding the net in the victory at St James' Park. Spurs would only confirm their league safety on the final day of the season.

SUNDAY 11th JANUARY 2009

Jermain Defoe fails to score on his second debut for Spurs as Maynor Figueroa's stoppage-time goal gives Wigan Athletic a 1-0 win at the JJB Stadium. It's the first time Defoe has failed to score a goal in his first game and the defeat leaves Spurs just two points off the bottom and in the thick of a relegation battle.

SATURDAY 12th JANUARY 1935

Spurs beat FA Cup holders Manchester City 1-0 in the FA Cup third-round tie at White Hart Lane. It's a bitter blow for City. It's no great surprise given the Blues' recent history at the Lane with City losing seven and drawing one of their last nine visits. Spurs also won the last meeting in north London 5-1, so the home support leave the ground not entirely surprised by events on the pitch.

MONDAY 12th JANUARY 1953

After holding Tranmere Rovers to a draw at Prenton Park in an FA Cup first-round replay, Spurs score a staggering nine goals in the White Hart Lane replay. Sid McClellan's hat-trick would have been more than enough to see the team through, but Len Duquemin, Roy Hollis and Eddie Baily score two goals each to send the Wirral side home with a 9-1 drubbing.

SATURDAY 13th JANUARY 1923

Midland League outfit Worksop Town come to White Hart Lane in the FA Cup and leave with a very credible draw. Spurs had been semi-finalists the year before and even included six of the side that had won the competition just two years earlier as a mark of respect for their lowly opponents, but they still couldn't get one over the Nottinghamshire club. The replay, staged just two days later – again at White Hart Lane – sees Spurs shift through the gears in an emphatic 9-0 victory.

SATURDAY 14th JANUARY 1978

A John Pratt brace, and a Colin Lee goal, earn Spurs a point against Notts County, as they look to return to the top flight at the first time of asking. Tottenham then embark on a 19-game unbeaten run, which aids a successful promotion campaign.

MONDAY 15th JANUARY 1923

Worksop's Town ground was deemed unfit to host the might of Tottenham Hotspur, which meant the replay between the two sides was to be once again played in north London. The visitors kept the same XI that started the original match, but they didn't have the same effect, as Spurs ran out victorious by scoring nine goals without reply. Alec Lindsay scores four times, with Tich Handley notching a hat-trick, whilst Jimmy Seed and Jimmy Dimmock net a goal each.

WEDNESDAY 16th JANUARY 1963

After 14 games unbeaten in the FA Cup, Spurs finally lose as Burnley progress in the competition after a 3-0 win. Nine of the starting XI from the previous year's cup-winning side were on duty that day, but they were powerless to resist the buoyant Clarets who were dominant and fully deserved their White Hart Lane triumph.

WEDNESDAY 17th JANUARY 1968

Martin Chivers makes his debut for Spurs after signing for a record £125,000. Jimmy Greaves equalises on the stroke of half-time with the game at Hillsborough seemingly heading for a draw, before Chivers scores the winner against Sheffield Wednesday to ensure a 2-1 win for Spurs, which was also their first victory at the ground since 1937.

FRIDAY 18th JANUARY 1965

The rearranged replay against fourth-division Torquay United proves a successful outing for Spurs, as they defeat their lowly rivals 5-1 thanks to a Jimmy Greaves treble and strikes from Alan Gilzean and Jimmy Robertson. It's the Lilywhites' first FA Cup victory since winning the competition three years earlier.

TUESDAY 18th JANUARY 2011

South African midfielder Steven Pienaar joins the club from Everton on a four-year-deal. A fee of around £3m was paid for his services as manager Harry Redknapp looks to provide an extra dimension to the club's engine room. Pienaar makes his debut in a 1-1 draw away at Newcastle and goes on to make another seven appearances in the league that season.

THURSDAY 19th JANUARY 1967

German midfielder Steffen Freund is born in Brandenburg. The tough-tackling anchor man became a cult hero with the Spurs faithful, thanks to his never-say-die attitude and no-nonsense approach to the game. Before signing for Spurs he had won the Champions League with Borussia Dortmund. He arrived in England in 1998 and played over 100 games for Spurs but never scored a competitive goal in a Tottenham shirt – despite the crowd urging him to 'shoot!' at almost every opportunity during the latter stages of his time at the Lane. Freund was inducted into the club's Hall of Fame in 2009 in recognition for his service to the club.

TUESDAY 19th JANUARY 1994

The first penalty shoot-out to take place at White Hart Lane is an intense affair as Spurs take on Peterborough United in an FA Cup replay. Nick Barmby's early strike was cancelled out by the Posh and the scores stayed level throughout normal and extra time, forcing the game to spot kicks. With Spurs scoring all of their penalties from 12 yards, their progression was confirmed when Ian Walker makes the only save of the shoot-out.

SATURDAY 20th JANUARY 1951

Top of the league and on course to win their first top-flight title, White Hart Lane was packed to the rafters as Wolves came to north London to take on Spurs. The hosts take maximum points thanks to goals from Sid McClellan and Sonny Walters that ultimately prove enough in a hard-fought 2-1 win.

WEDNESDAY 20th JANUARY 2010

Dirk Kuyt scores twice to boost Liverpool's hopes of Champions League football in a 2-0 win over top-four rivals Spurs at Anfield. The Dutch striker scores after six minutes and seals the points with an injury-time penalty to close the gap on Harry Redknapp's men to just one point.

WEDNESDAY 21st JANUARY 1976

A League Cup semi-final meant Spurs could lift the gloom that had enveloped the club in recent seasons, but sadly, it wasn't to be, as Newcastle triumphed 3-1 at St James' Park. Tottenham led 1-0 from the first leg and though Don McAllister gave the Lilywhites a chance with a goal, it was not enough and the Magpies went on to face Manchester City at Wembley – losing 2-1 to the Blues on the day.

SATURDAY 22nd JANUARY 1955

Sheffield Wednesday arrive at White Hart Lane to play on a mud bath of a pitch. The home side adapt to the conditions better, finding the net on no less than seven occasions, including a goal from Jonny Gavin in the very first minute. Spurs add six more thanks to George Robb, Len Duquemin, Eddie Baily and two from George Brooks. Gavin also scores again in this embarrassingly one-sided game.

TUESDAY 22nd JANUARY 2008

Having drawn the first leg 1-1 at the Emirates, Tottenham run riot against Arsenal in the second leg to book a place in the League Cup Final. Spurs get off to the perfect start when Jermaine Jenas scores after just three minutes and White Hart Lane erupts when Nicklas Bendtner heads into his own net before Robbie Keane makes it three just after the break. Aaron Lennon scores a fourth and although Emmanuel Adebayor grabs a consolation for Arsenal, Steed Malbranque adds a fifth on 90 minutes to send Spurs through to the League Cup Final.

WEDNESDAY 23rd JANUARY 2002

A stunning five-star display sees Spurs brush aside Chelsea in the second leg of their League Cup semi-final clash. Steffen Iversen and Tim Sherwood put Spurs two up before half-time, with Teddy Sheringham, Simon Davies and Sergei Rebrov making sure Chelsea lose at White Hart Lane for the first time since 1987. Unfortunately, Spurs are unable to take the momentum into the League Cup Final, where Blackburn Rovers triumph.

SATURDAY 24th JANUARY 1981

The mesmeric midfield duo of Glenn Hoddle and Ossie Ardiles are too much for third-division Hull City, as the talented pair give the Tigers the run around in this FA Cup fourth-round clash. Numerous chances are created with Steve Archibald and Garth Crooks on target in a 2-0 win.

WEDNESDAY 24th JANUARY 2007

Spurs throw away a 2-0 lead against Arsenal in the League Cup semi-final first leg at White Hart Lane. Dimitar Berbatov puts the hosts ahead on 12 minutes and an own goal from the Gunners' Julio Baptista doubles Martin Jol's side's advantage on 21 minutes. But it is Baptista who dominates after the break, scoring on 64 and 77 minutes to complete an unlikely draw and shift the tie's advantage to Arsenal.

SATURDAY 25th JANUARY 1964

Derek Possee scores on his debut as Spurs inflict a 3-1 defeat on Aston Villa. The winger had replaced the injured Cliff Jones in what was an aging side going through a period of transition. Jimmy Greaves and Terry Dyson add the other goals as Spurs earn two more points.

TUESDAY 25th JANUARY 1967

The enigmatic David Ginola is born in Gassin, France. The immensely talented winger played for Paris St Germain and Newcastle United before signing for Spurs in 1997 for £2.5m. He went on to play 100 league games for the club, finding the net on 13 occasions. Ginola was immensely popular with the Spurs fans because of his style and panache, though his talents made little impact on the French national team, following a falling out with boss Gérard Houllier. Following Les Bleus' failure to qualify for the 1994 World Cup, manager Houllier blamed Ginola personally for their elimination. Ginola departed White Hart Lane in 2000 to sign for Aston Villa, though he is still fondly remembered by his legion of fans in north London.

WEDNESDAY 25th JANUARY 1995

Jurgen Klinsmann is knocked unconscious by Aston Villa keeper Mark Bosnich and lies motionless on the ground for four minutes before being stretchered off. To add insult to serious injury, Spurs lose the game by a single goal.

SUNDAY 26th JANUARY 1919

No-one could have known that when William Edward Nicholson was born in Scarborough, he would become Tottenham's greatest manager of all time. Nicholson signed for Spurs as a 16-year-old and went on to play 314 times for the club, before taking on the role of manager in 1958. It only took him a couple of years to stamp his name into the club's history books when his Spurs side won the First Division championship and FA Cup – the much-coveted 'Double'. Nicholson resigned in 1974 and spent time as an advisor at West Ham United, before returning to his beloved White Hart Lane to perform a similar role at the club. He died in 2004.

SATURDAY 26th JANUARY 1991

Paul Gascoigne has one of his most impressive displays in a Spurs shirt as the Lilywhites take on Oxford United in an FA Cup tie. Gazza's powers are at their peak as he terrorises the visitors, scoring twice and totally dominating the game with his individual brilliance. Gary Lineker and Gary Mabbutt make sure of Spurs' passage into the next round, both adding a goal in what was a comfortable afternoon for the Lilywhites.

ENIGMATIC FRENCH WINGER DAVID GINOLA – SEEN HERE SHOWING OFF THE LEAGUE CUP – WAS BORN IN JANUARY 1967.

WEDNESDAY 26th JANUARY 1994

After 97 appearances and 22 goals for Liverpool, popular Israeli striker Ronny Rosenthal joins Spurs for £250,000. Rosenthal had slipped out of the first-team picture during the 1994/95 campaign and some supporters – mostly at other clubs – couldn't forget his astonishing miss away to Aston Villa when he thundered a shot against the bar from a few yards out. Ironically, his transfer went through just 48 hours before Graeme Souness resigned as Liverpool boss, but it was two days too late for Ronny. Rosenthal scores 11 goals in 100 appearances during his time at the Lane.

SATURDAY 27th JANUARY 1968

Martin Chivers scores twice as Spurs gain a credible 2-2 draw at Old Trafford in the FA Cup. Tottenham took the lead in the fourth minute, but found themselves behind by the middle of the second half. Spurs looked to be heading out of the competition until Chivers got his second in the very last minute of the match. Spurs edge the White Hart Lane replay 1-0 four days later.

SATURDAY 28th JANUARY 1961

Crewe Alexandra – The Railwaymen – attempt to derail Spurs at White Hart Lane in the fourth round of the FA Cup. Five goals from Spurs, however, see Crewe shunted and the Lilywhites into the fifth round of the FA Cup. Terry Dyson, Bobby Smith, Dave MacKay, Cliff Jones and Les Allen were all on the score-sheet.

SATURDAY 28th JANUARY 1984

Norwich City earn a replay after the FA Cup fourth-round tie at White Hart Lane ends 0-0. The Canaries complete the job at Carrow Road with a 2-1 win and passage into the last 16.

SUNDAY 28th JANUARY 2007

Former Dutch international Edgar Davids leaves Spurs to re-sign for this first club Ajax. The European Cup winner played 40 times for the Lilywhites during his 18-month spell, before returning to his homeland. He only scored once for Tottenham, but his level head in midfield was a key factor in the club's two fifth-place Premier League finishes in Davids' time with the club.

MONDAY 28th JANUARY 2008

England defender Jonathan Woodgate arrives at White Hart Lane for a fee of £7m from Middlesbrough. The England international is an instant hit with the fans due to his elegant play at the back, but the former Leeds United and Real Madrid man would struggle with injuries – as he had throughout his career – during his time at the club, limiting him to only 49 league appearances in over three years. He failed to agree terms on a new deal, and departed on a free transfer in the summer of 2011 to sign for Stoke City.

SATURDAY 29th JANUARY 1910

Over a century ago, Spurs were enjoying their second season in the Football League and on this particular day, created a little piece of history with a starting XI that contained three brothers for the first time in the club's history. Bobby, Danny and Alex Steel were all on the team sheet for the goalless draw against Bradford. It was to be right-back Alex's only appearance for Spurs.

SATURDAY 30th JANUARY 1960

A trip to Gresty Road leads to a 2-2 draw in the FA Cup. Crewe dominated the game, and if it wasn't for the impressive Spurs goalkeeper Bill Brown, the south Cheshire outfit would have almost certainly progressed. Cliff Jones and Les Allen scored for Tottenham as they successfully avoided an embarrassing upset to fight another day.

WEDNESDAY 31st JANUARY 1968

Two red cards were the main talking points in a colourful FA Cup replay against Manchester United as Joe Kinnear and Brian Kidd were sent off. It took until extra time for the game to be decided as Jimmy Robertson scored a disputed goal for Tottenham, with the Red Devils claiming that Mike England had fouled Reds' keeper Alex Stepney in the build-up to the goal. The ref, however, was having none of it!

SATURDAY 31st JANUARY 2001

West Ham United and Spurs play out a dull 0-0 draw at Upton Park. The draw does little to enhance the cause of either side who remain firmly rooted in mid-table.

SATURDAY 31st JANUARY 2004

Robbie Keane's 18th-minute penalty gives Spurs a 1-0 lead at Craven Cottage, but Fulham recover to take all three points in a disappointing London derby. Keane's goal came after Ian Pearce handled in the box but the Cottagers converted a penalty of their own on the stroke of half-time when future Tottenham star Steed Malbranque slotted home. There was worse to come after the break when the opposition's new signing Brian McBride scored what proved to be the winning goal on 67 minutes, lobbing Kasey Keller to cap an impressive debut.

TUESDAY 31st JANUARY 2006

Fulham continue their hoodoo over Spurs with a fourth successive victory at Craven Cottage. Carlos Bocanegra's 90th-minute goal proves enough to give the hosts the three points and maintain their scintillating home form in the process. The defeat does little for Spurs' Champions League hopes, although they remain in fourth place in the Premier League, three points ahead of nearest challengers Wigan Athletic.

WEDNESDAY 31st JANUARY 2007

Spurs pay the price for giving away a two-goal advantage in the first leg as Arsenal progress to the League Cup Final. In the second leg at the Emirates Stadium, the Gunners appeared to have done enough when Emmanuel Adebayor put the hosts 1-0 up on 77 minutes but Egyptian striker Mido equalised for the Lilywhites on 85 minutes to force the game into extra time. Unfortunately, Jeremie Aliadiere, and an own goal from Pascal Chimbonda, give Arsene Wenger's side a 3-1 victory on the night – 5-3 on aggregate – to progress to the final.

SATURDAY 31st JANUARY 2009

Two second-half Darren Bent goals are not enough to prevent Spurs losing in a thrilling five-goal encounter away to Bolton Wanderers. The Trotters went 1-0 up before the break courtesy of Sebastien Puygrenier's 34th-minute goal and new skipper Kevin Davies makes it 2-0 just past the hour. Second-half sub Darren Bent has other ideas, however, and looks to have earned Harry Redknapp's side a point with goals on 73 and 75 minutes. In fact, Spurs sniff all three points before Davies strikes again on 87 minutes to seal three points for the Reebok Stadium-based club.

SPURS
On This Day

FEBRUARY

SATURDAY 1st FEBRUARY 2003

Spurs collect a rare point away to Chelsea – the first for eight years. Teddy Sheringham puts the visitors ahead, but they are pegged back when a superb Gianfranco Zola free kick beats Kasey Keller five minutes before the break in a game that could easily have finished 4-4. The draw keeps Spurs on level points with sixth-placed Liverpool.

TUESDAY 1st FEBRUARY 2005

After getting the New Year off to a flier with a 5-2 win over Everton, Tottenham Hotspur had a slight dip in form, and it continued as they travelled north to face Bolton Wanderers, who ran out 3-1 winners. All of the goals came in the second half, with El-Hadji Diouf opening the scoring with a penalty just four minutes after the re-start. Jermain Defoe equalised with a quarter of the game remaining, but the turning point came when Frederic Kanoute was shown a second yellow card just two minutes later. The Trotters had to wait until the last five minutes before securing victory, with Tal Ben-Haim and Kevin Davies scoring two goals in as many minutes to compound Spurs' misery.

SATURDAY 2nd FEBRUARY 1985

A crowd of 17,511 fans watch Luton Town and Tottenham Hotspur share the spoils at Kenilworth Road in a Division One clash. Defender Graham Roberts, who was part of the club's Uefa Cup-winning squad, gets Spurs' first goal of the game – his eighth goal of the campaign – but it's nip and tuck with the Hatters and though Mark Falco nets his 21st goal of the season, points are shared in a tight encounter in Bedfordshire.

MONDAY 2nd FEBRUARY 1987

In times gone by teams were forced to play out replays when League Cup games were drawn. In this game, Tottenham made up for lost opportunities in the first match, by despatching West Ham United 5-0 at White Hart Lane. Nico Claesen opens the scoring with Glenn Hoddle adding a second. In the final ten minutes, Spurs striker Clive Allen somehow manages to bag a hat-trick to complete the rout.

MONDAY 2nd FEBRUARY 2009

Robbie Keane returns to the club only six months after leaving for Liverpool. The Irishman never settled in the north-west after moving to Anfield for £20m in the summer. Tottenham were failing to fire, so Harry Redknapp decided to bring Keane back to White Hart Lane when the opportunity arose. In his first spell at Spurs he scored an impressive 80 goals in 197 league appearances, but only found the net once every four games second time around. After two loan spells away from Spurs, he was eventually sold to LA Galaxy in August 2011.

WEDNESDAY 3rd FEBRUARY 1960

It is rare to hear of a 15-goal game, but when Crewe visited White Hart Lane in an FA Cup replay, that is exactly what happened. Unfortunately, for the away side they conceded 13 in 90 minutes with Spurs 10-1 up by half-time. Les Allen scored five on the day with Bobby Smith netting four times. This is still the club's biggest win – a 13-2 record victory.

SATURDAY 3rd FEBRUARY 1973

The FA Cup fourth-round tie between Derby County and Tottenham Hotspur ends in a 1-1 draw at the Baseball Ground. Martin Chivers was on target for Spurs to force a replay at White Hart Lane, which the Rams went on to win 5-3 after extra time – Chivers scored on that night too. Derby lost at the quarter-final stage to eventual runners-up Leeds United, who famously lost 1-0 in the final to Sunderland, courtesy of an Ian Porterfield goal.

SATURDAY 4th FEBRUARY 1961

In a season remembered for Spurs doing the 'double', the club still had a few glitches along the way, including this 3-2 home defeat at the hands of Leicester City. Les Allen and Danny Blanchflower had twice equalised for Tottenham, before the Foxes scored the killer goal in the second half, with champions-elect Spurs unable to snatch a point. It was the Lilywhites' first home defeat of the season having previously only dropped two points in 13 games, but Bill Nicholson's team were still eight points clear at the top.

WEDNESDAY 4th FEBRUARY 2004

Spurs are on the wrong end of one of the greatest comebacks in FA Cup history when ten-man Manchester City come from three goals behind to win a fourth-round replay at White Hart Lane. Tottenham went ahead thanks to goals from Ledley King, Robbie Keane and Christian Ziege. They were aided when the referee sent off Joey Barton for dissent at half-time. However, the visitors fought back against all the odds, scoring four times through Sylvain Distin, Paul Bosvelt, Shaun Wright-Phillips and Jon Macken to progress to the next round.

SUNDAY 4th FEBRUARY 2007

Manchester United stroll to a comfortable victory at White Hart Lane in a game that would prove to be Spurs' biggest defeat of the season. Cristiano Ronaldo got the ball rolling when he converted a penalty on the stroke of half-time and the second period proved to be a one-sided affair, too, as Nemanja Vidic, Paul Scholes and Ryan Giggs helped United to a resounding 4-0 victory.

WEDNESDAY 5th FEBRUARY 1986

With English teams banned from Europe, clubs were entered into a makeshift competition called the Screen Sport Super Cup. Spurs reached the semi-finals but the fans gave the competition a massive thumbs-down. Only 7,548 attended the first-leg clash with Everton, which ended 0-0, and the Toffees took the second leg 3-1 at Goodison Park to progress to the final against Liverpool. The competition, like numerous others that have been dreamed up over the years, died after just one season with the public's apathy, and the fact there was no Wembley final to aim for, the main reasons for its demise.

SUNDAY 5th FEBRUARY 1995

Tottenham Hotspur beat eventual Premier League champions Blackburn Rovers 3-1 at White Hart Lane, with soon-to-be Spurs midfielder Tim Sherwood getting the visitors' only goal. Jurgen Klinsmann scores his 18th goal of the season, while Darren Anderton bags his fourth of the campaign. Nick Barmby seals victory for Spurs with his eighth goal in all competitions to round off a fine performance for Gerry Francis' team.

JURGEN KLINSMANN FIRES GOAL NUMBER 18 OF THE 1994/95 SEASON.

SATURDAY 6th FEBRUARY 1971

Manchester United scrape a 2-1 victory at Old Trafford to dent Tottenham Hotspur's slim Division One title hopes. Martin Peters scores Spurs' only goal of the game, but it was not enough to overcome a strong United side. Nearly 48,500 fans squeezed into Old Trafford to watch this closely-contested game between two of the best sides in England at the time. Spurs went on to finish third in the league under the charge of Bill Nicholson, but found glory not long after this game in the League Cup, beating Aston Villa 2-0 at Wembley.

SATURDAY 6th FEBRUARY 1982

The new West Stand is officially opened as Wolverhampton Wanderers visit White Hart Lane and those who witnessed the game from this new vantage point were not to be disappointed; Tottenham win 6-1 with Ricky Villa grabbing the headlines with a hat-trick. Glenn Hoddle helps himself to a penalty, before Garth Crooks and Mark Falco round off the scoring late on against the eventually relegated Wolves.

THURSDAY 7th FEBRUARY 1935

One of Spurs' finest ever players, Cliff Jones, is born in Swansea. The winger started his career with his hometown club, where his talent didn't go unnoticed in England's capital as Tottenham brought him to north London in 1958 as one of the final pieces in Bill Nicholson's jigsaw. In his time with the club, he managed to win five major honours, including three FA Cups, as well as earning 59 caps for his country. He played for a decade at White Hart Lane, before moving across London to Fulham where he enjoyed a short spell. Jones would play for a variety of clubs as his career wound down, and also gained 59 caps for Wales.

WEDNESDAY 7th FEBRUARY 1973

Spurs were cruising to the sixth round of the FA Cup as they led Derby County 3-1 going into the last ten minutes of extra time thanks to goals from Martin Chivers, Alan Gilzean and Mike England, but they went on to concede a Roger Davies hat-trick as the Rams turned the game on its head, and progressed to the next round.

SUNDAY 7th FEBRUARY 1993

Just over 20,000 fans watch as Tottenham Hotspur beat Southampton at White Hart Lane. Teddy Sheringham scores twice to take his tally to 15 for the season. Darren Anderton scores only his second goal of the season – his first in the league – and Nick Barmby nets his seventh goal of the campaign as Spurs run out 4-2 winners in the Premier League fixture. The same three players were on the score-sheet just seven days later in an FA Cup fifth-round tie, as Spurs beat Wimbledon 3-2. The win over the Saints eases relegation fears for Spurs while compounding Southampton's who are left just five points off the bottom.

SUNDAY 8th FEBRUARY 1987

Clive Allen's 34th goal of the campaign gives Spurs a crucial lead in the first leg of the Littlewoods Cup semi-final against Arsenal. Spurs thoroughly deserve their victory as they dominate the majority of the match and were unfortunate not to add to their tally.

SATURDAY 8th FEBRUARY 2003

Teddy Sheringham rounds off the scoring as Tottenham Hotspur run out comprehensive winners against Sunderland at White Hart Lane. The England international scores his ninth goal of the season with just six minutes left to play, adding to the goals from Gustavo Poyet, Gary Doherty and Simon Davies, as Spurs ease to victory in the Premier League fixture. Kevin Phillips had equalised for the visitors in the first half, but from that moment on, it was one-way traffic. The win moves Spurs up to seventh while the Black Cats remain rooted to the foot of the Premier League.

SATURDAY 9th FEBRUARY 1901

Preston North End visit White Hart Lane for the first FA Cup tie at Tottenham's sparkling new home. Despite going a goal behind, Spurs fight back and equalise through Sandy Brown, which made sure that both teams would get a second chance to progress to the next round. The game had been delayed from its original date due to the death of Queen Victoria.

SATURDAY 9th FEBRUARY 1980

Tottenham Hotspur collapse to defeat at the hands of West Bromwich Albion in a Division One clash. Glenn Hoddle scores his 15th goal of the campaign, but it was not enough as the Baggies net two of their own to condemn Spurs to defeat at The Hawthorns. It was another loss in a disappointing season for Spurs, who finish a lowly 14th under the charge of Keith Burkinshaw – one point behind West Brom.

WEDNESDAY 10th FEBRUARY 1926

Robert Dennis Blanchflower is born in Belfast. More commonly known as Danny by his friends, and adoring fans, the midfielder became a Tottenham legend after signing from Aston Villa in 1954. He was the heartbeat of the club's most successful ever team. Blanchflower was a two-time winner of the Football Writers' Player of the Year, but he will be more fondly remembered for the trophies he led the team to, as Spurs claimed the double in 1961 by winning the league championship and FA Cup, the latter he would win once more the following year. Additionally, he made 56 appearances for Northern Ireland, and would later manage the country of his birth. He died in 1993.

SATURDAY 10th FEBRUARY 2001

Spurs were on a fine run as they arrived at Maine Road to take on Manchester City; the Lilywhites hadn't conceded a goal in the previous four games and continued that run as they returned to north London with all three points. Sergei Rebrov scored the winner in the 89th minute, to give Tottenham their first away victory of the season.

TUESDAY 10th FEBRUARY 2004

Goals from Simon Davies, Jermain Defoe and Ledley King give Tottenham Hotspur a 3-0 lead against Charlton Athletic, but goals from Graham Stuart and Chris Perry ensure a nervy finish at The Valley. However, an 85th-minute strike from Jonny Jackson, his first goal of the season, sealed the points for Spurs who made the short trip back to north London with three points in the bag. It was the second of three consecutive Premier League games during which the club scores four goals.

ONE OF THE GREATEST SPURS PLAYERS OF ALL TIME DANNY BLANCHFLOWER – BORN IN FEBRUARY 1926 – PICTURED WITH BOBBY SMITH AND JIMMY GREAVES.

SATURDAY 11th FEBRUARY 1928

Top-of-the-league Everton were no match for Spurs at Goodison Park, as the visitors came away with a 5-2 victory. Jimmy Dimmock and Eugene O'Callaghan put Tottenham two goals ahead early on, but it was O'Callaghan who would grab the headlines as he went on to add three more goals, to give him four on the day.

SATURDAY 11th FEBRUARY 1967

Goals from Alan Gilzean and Jimmy Greaves are cancelled out by Fulham before half-time. The first period also saw the dismissal of Terry Venables and a Fulham player following an altercation. After the break Tottenham took charge, with winger Cliff Jones scoring twice to ensure victory for the men from White Hart Lane.

SATURDAY 11th FEBRUARY 1989

Former Manchester City midfielder Paul Stewart scores Spurs' only goal as they only manage a 1-1 draw with Charlton Athletic at White Hart Lane. It was the last of five disappointing Division One results since the turn of the year, in which Spurs only picked up two points and were even dumped out of the FA Cup in the third round by Second Division outfit Bradford City, 1-0 at Valley Parade.

SATURDAY 12th FEBRUARY 1966

With the side trailing by two goals against Burnley in the fourth round of the FA Cup, Spurs find the belly for a fightback. Alan Gilzean scores a hat-trick, with Frank Saul adding another, to give Spurs a 4-3 win. The next Lancastrian outfit they meet in the fifth round sees the Lilywhites lose to another club nicknamed the Lilywhites – Preston North End.

SATURDAY 12th FEBRUARY 2005

Strikers Jermain Defoe and Robbie Keane rescue Spurs with goals to send the club through to the fifth round of the FA Cup at the expense of West Bromwich Albion. Nigeria international Nwankwo Kanu gave the visitors the lead in the replay at White Hart Lane, but Defoe scores an equaliser on the stroke of half-time to ease manager Martin Jol's team talk. Two goals in ten second-half minutes from Robbie Keane secure safe passage to the next round.

WEDNESDAY 13th FEBRUARY 1901

Spurs go into their FA Cup replay against Preston North End as underdogs, with non-league Lilywhites given little hope of defeating the First Division giants. Manager John Cameron nets the opening goal with Sandy Brown adding a hat-trick to give Spurs a 4-2 win over the Deepdale outfit to send shockwaves through English football that a new power was emerging in north London.

SATURDAY 13th FEBRUARY 1982

Home-grown striker Mark Falco scores the only goal of the game as Spurs beat Aston Villa 1-0 in an FA Cup fifth-round tie at White Hart Lane. This victory follows 1-0 wins over Arsenal and Leeds United in the third and fourth round, respectively, to set up a quarter-final tie with Chelsea which Keith Burkinshaw's focused side also win. Spurs go on to win the competition for the second consecutive season, after beating Queens Park Rangers in a replay.

SATURDAY 14th FEBRUARY 1953

A trip to the claustrophobic confines of The Shay, home of Halifax Town, was never the easiest of away trips so it was understandable that Spurs approached this game with some trepidation as they travelled up to West Yorkshire. Snowy conditions made it even harder for Tottenham, and the hosts gave their all in the first half, going in on equal terms at the break. The second 45 minutes was a different story with Spurs scoring three times as Les Bennett bags a brace, and Len Duquemin nets once, as the Lilywhites chased more silverware.

THURSDAY 14th FEBRUARY 2008

Juande Ramos' team picks up a crucial win in the Czech Republic to keep their Uefa Cup dream alive. First-half strikes from Bulgaria international Dimitar Berbatov and Republic of Ireland striker Robbie Keane give Spurs two vital away goals against Slavia Prague, who pull a goal back in the second half through David Strihavka to halve the deficit. Despite the hosts coming back strongly, the game ends in a crucial 2-1 victory for Ramos' men.

SUNDAY 15th FEBRUARY 1969

Record signing Roger Morgan had recently arrived from Queens Park Rangers for £110,000. He had played for the Rs for his entire career prior to the move, and was in the same side as his twin brother Ian at Loftus Road. His first appearance against his former club saw the teams share the spoils in a 1-1 draw as Jimmy Greaves nets Spurs' goal.

THURSDAY 15th FEBRUARY 1996

The FA Cup fifth-round tie between Nottingham Forest and Spurs is postponed due to heavy snow at the City Ground. The delay of Spurs' fifth FA Cup fixture of the season (having been held to draws by Hereford United and Wolverhampton Wanderers in the previous two rounds) was frustrating, but the game was re-scheduled a fortnight later – only to end in a 2-2 draw. It was Forest who went on to win the tie 3-1 courtesy of a penalty shoot-out after the two sides could not be separated after a further 120 minutes of football.

SATURDAY 16th FEBRUARY 1980

Glenn Hoddle scores twice for Spurs to help the club ease into the quarter-final of the FA Cup. The former England midfielder and manager took his tally to 15 for the season after he added to Gerry Armstrong's goal. It was the Northern Ireland international's last season at White Hart Lane.

SATURDAY 16th FEBRUARY 1992

Spurs lose the chance to move into the top ten after losing 1-0 to Crystal Palace at Selhurst Park. The win puts the Eagles in eighth spot, three points behind Chelsea and only four behind London's highest-placed team at that point, Arsenal.

TUESDAY 16th FEBRUARY 1999

A 1-0 win at Wimbledon in the second leg of the Worthington Cup semi was enough to ensure that Spurs made it to the final. Steffen Iversen's strike late on was the difference between the two teams on the night – and over the two games – after a goalless draw at White Hart Lane. The victory was met with a joyous pitch invasion when the final whistle blew.

FRIDAY 17th FEBRUARY 1899

John Cameron is appointed as Spurs manager. His role was not like that of the modern-day tacticians and coaches, as he elects to continue playing, while also performing the tasks of the club secretary. During his time in charge, the club won the Southern League and FA Cup. Cameron was a hugely popular figure with the fans and players alike, but decided to leave the job in 1907 to seek a fresh challenge.

SATURDAY 17th FEBRUARY 1951

Future England manager Alf Ramsey hits Tottenham's first goal in a 3-2 win over Aston Villa at White Hart Lane. The 1966 World Cup-winning boss scored a penalty, which was soon added to by Eddie Baily, who began his career at Spurs and spent ten years at the Lane before moving to Port Vale in 1956. The eventual winner was scored by winger Les Medley in front of a more-than-decent 47,842 crowd.

SATURDAY 17th FEBRUARY 1962

A pulsating, end-to-end cup tie at The Hawthorns is eventually won 4-2 by Spurs. The fifth-round game saw Bobby Smith score twice in the first half to set Tottenham on their way against an off-colour West Bromwich Albion. After the break, Jimmy Greaves also nets two goals, confirming Spurs' progression to the next round.

TUESDAY 18th FEBRUARY 1947

Burnley's hopes of going top are thwarted by a resilient Spurs at Turf Moor. The Clarets remain a point behind leaders Manchester City while Spurs move up two places to fifth in Division One.

WEDNESDAY 18th FEBRUARY 1959

Being the victim of a cup upset is something of a rarity for a club with the FA Cup pedigree Spurs have, but on this occasion they came off the worse when they took on Norwich City. After a draw at White Hart Lane, Spurs travelled to Norfolk to take on the Canaries where the home side scored the only goal of the game in the 63rd minute to give the Third Division (South) club a famous victory.

SATURDAY 18th FEBRUARY 1961

A goal from Cliff Jones puts Tottenham Hotspur on course for victory in an FA Cup fifth-round tie against Aston Villa. The Welshman nets his 12th goal of the season before Villa defender John Neal puts the ball into his own net to complete the scoring at Villa Park. It also sets up a quarter-final tie for Spurs with Sunderland. Bill Nicholson's team went on to win the competition, beating Leicester City 2-0 in the final, the third FA Cup triumph in Spurs' history.

SATURDAY 19th FEBRUARY 1972

Martin Chivers scores twice as Tottenham Hotspur ease to a 2-0 victory over Stoke City at White Hart Lane. The England international nets his 32nd and 33rd goals of the season respectively in what had already been a memorable campaign for the former Southampton striker, who goes on to score an astonishing 42 goals. He would go on to be the club's top scorer for a further two seasons, making it four in a row – a record bettered only by Jimmy Greaves.

SATURDAY 19th FEBRUARY 1983

A first loss in 19 FA Cup ties comes when Spurs visit Goodison Park. The club had won the two previous competitions. There were some extenuating circumstances on this occasion, with Spurs lacking many first-choice players due to injury, but the team still performed disappointingly as they lost 2-0 to Everton.

SATURDAY 20th FEBRUARY 1993

With Leeds United unbeaten at Elland Road, Spurs face a tough trip north in the inaugural year of the Premier League. While Leeds boast the worst away record in the top flight, they are the only side not to lose on home soil – until this game as Spurs score four goals without reply in a stunning performance. Fans' favourite Teddy Sheringham puts the Lilywhites two up before half-time, with Neil Ruddock making it three, before Sheringham adds a fourth to earn the first hat-trick of his Tottenham career. The win takes the Lilywhites to within three points of fourth spot.

CLIFF JONES SCORED FOR SPURS IN THE FA CUP WIN OVER ASTON VILLA IN FEBRUARY 1961.

WEDNESDAY 21st FEBRUARY 1979

Striker Chris Jones scores a hat-trick for Spurs in an FA Cup replay at Wrexham to give the club a welcome distraction from their disappointing campaign in the league. Jones' three goals were the difference in the 3-2 victory over the energetic and hardworking Welsh outfit.

TUESDAY 21st FEBRUARY 1984

Striker Steve Archibald scores Tottenham's first goal of the game in a 3-2 victory over Leicester City at White Hart Lane. Mark Falco adds Spurs' second before Tony Galvin nets what proves to be the winner. Galvin was brought to north London by manager Keith Burkinshaw from Northern Premier Division outfit Goole, and was a key player during his nine years with Tottenham during which time he made 273 appearances and scored 31 goals.

SUNDAY 21st FEBRUARY 2010

Jermain Defoe scores his sixth goal of the campaign against Wigan Athletic as Tottenham Hotspur ease to a 3-0 victory at the DW Stadium. The England international put five past the Latics when the sides met at White Hart Lane in a 9-0 thrashing earlier in the season and the striker picks up where he left off with the opening goal of this fixture. It was Defoe's 22nd goal of the campaign. Russian striker Roman Pavlyuchenko adds two more – his third and fourth goals of the season. Crucially, the win puts Spurs back into fourth spot above Manchester City in the battle for Champions League football.

WEDNESDAY 22nd FEBRUARY 1933

Bobby Smith is born in Lingdale, North Yorkshire. The strong centre forward started his playing career at Chelsea at the age of 17. He arrived at White Hart Lane in 1955 and his scoring record would ensure his hero status with the club's fans. Smith found the net on 176 occasions in 271 league games during his nine years with the club. It was no coincidence that this mirrored Spurs' most successful ever period. He only earned 15 caps for his country, but still managed 13 international goals. Smith died in 2010.

MONDAY 22nd FEBRUARY 1937

A waterlogged pitch means that the FA Cup replay against Everton at White Hart Lane was a difficult, and at times treacherous, encounter for both teams. The Toffees adapt quicker and take a two-goal lead in the first period, before Spurs pulled one back through Johnny Morrison. Everton quickly regain their two-goal advantage and lead 3-1 until seven minutes from time when Morrison adds a second. Joe Meek then equalises before Morrison completes his hat-trick with a dramatic late winner to give Spurs a famous 4-3 victory.

SATURDAY 22nd FEBRUARY 1964

Very few players make the move down the Seven Sisters Road from Arsenal to Spurs, but one who did was Laurie Brown. He arrived at White Hart Lane for a fee of £40,000. By a strange twist of fate, the centre-half made his Spurs debut in a north London derby against his former employers. It seemed that he had obviously made the right choice as Spurs won 3-1. He played another 61 times for the club, before leaving for Norwich City.

WEDNESDAY 22nd FEBRUARY 1978

Glenn Hoddle scores twice for Keith Burkinshaw's Tottenham Hotspur side who blow Luton Town away with a scintillating display of attacking football. Defender Don McAllister even gets on the score-sheet during the 4-1 thrashing, while forward John Duncan grabs Spurs' other goal in an impressive display at Kenilworth Road. The result would help the club reach third in Division Two, ultimately clinching promotion ahead of Brighton & Hove Albion on goal difference. Spurs scored the most goals out of any club in the top three divisions that season (83). The only teams who scored more were Division Four teams: Swansea City (87), Brentford (86) and Watford (85) – all of whom were promoted.

SATURDAY 23rd FEBRUARY 1901

In Spurs' early days as a non-league side they caused a few FA Cup upsets, including a 2-1 win against Bury. The Lancastrian side dominated throughout, with Spurs only being kept in the match thanks to some inspirational goalkeeping from George Clawley. The Lilywhites go a goal down, but Sandy Brown equalises and then goes on to score the winner to complete the turnaround.

SATURDAY 23rd FEBRUARY 1963

Bill Nicholson's Tottenham scrape a priceless victory against fierce rivals Arsenal in the north London derby. Tony Marchi got the first goal for Spurs, one of only a handful the wing-half got during two spells at the club. Centre forward Bobby Smith scored only his third goal of the season as he added a second goal for Tottenham, before winger Cliff Jones scored what proved to be the winner in front of nearly 60,000 people at Highbury. It was an impressive campaign for Spurs, who finished second behind Everton, who claimed the English championship for the sixth time. Tottenham scored 111 goals in the league that year – 30 of which came in just six games between September 29th 1962 and November 3rd 1962.

SATURDAY 24th FEBRUARY 1934

Spurs take a hard-earned point at Fratton Park in a 0-0 draw with Portsmouth. The draw keeps fourth-placed Tottenham on the trail of leaders Arsenal who are six points better off.

MONDAY 24th FEBRUARY 1997

Teddy Sheringham gets Spurs off to the best possible start at Upton Park, but Gerry Francis' team show their defensive frailties once more as West Ham United recover to win 4-3 in the Premier League. Two goals in as many minutes from Julian Dicks and Paul Kitson puts the Hammers in front, but Darren Anderton pulls Spurs level just before the half-hour mark. John Hartson puts the hosts back in front to complete the scoring for the first half. David Howells gets Spurs' second equaliser of the game before Dicks nets the winner from the penalty spot on 72 minutes to secure victory for West Ham.

SUNDAY 24th FEBRUARY 2002

With silverware in their sights, Glenn Hoddle's side arrives at the Millennium Stadium feeling confident that they could leave with the League Cup. The opposition on the day is Blackburn Rovers, who were unflustered by the occasion, proving as much by taking the lead through Matt Jansen, before Christian Ziege equalises. Then, on 68 minutes, a rare Ledley King mistake lets Andy Cole in for what proves to be the winner for Rovers and gives the Ewood Park club their first trophy for 74 years to end Hoddle's dream.

SUNDAY 24th FEBRUARY 2008

Spurs face Chelsea in the League Cup Final. The West London outfit begin strong favourites thanks mainly to their league position and past record against Tottenham. The bookies seem to have got it right, too, when Chelsea take the lead in the first half when Didier Drogba fires home a 20-yard free kick that leaves the keeper helpless. A Dimitar Berbatov penalty brings the scores level with 20 minutes left on the clock but neither side can find a winner in normal time so an extra 30 minutes is played. Before five minutes had elapsed of extra time Jonathan Woodgate wrote himself in Tottenham folklore by flicking in a header to give Juande Ramos' Spurs team a hugely satisfying victory.

THURSDAY 25th FEBRUARY 1904

After a match against Aston Villa was abandoned due to a half-time pitch invasion at White Hart Lane with the visitors a goal ahead, the sides were forced to replay at Villa Park. Despite being fined for the fracas, it worked out well for Spurs in the end as they defeated Villa on their home turf with 'Bristol' Jones scoring the winner.

WEDNESDAY 25th FEBRUARY 1987

Spurs record their biggest league win of the campaign as they thrash Leicester City 5-0 in a Division One clash. Clive Allen, Paul Allen and Nico Claesen were all on the score-sheet as David Pleat's side ran out comprehensive winners in a one-sided game at White Hart Lane. Just three weeks earlier, Spurs had beaten West Ham United in a League Cup fifth-round tie 5-0, and were in a rich vein of form, having also overcome Arsenal and Southampton before easing past the Foxes.

MONDAY 26th FEBRUARY 1962

A goal behind from the first leg, Spurs had to draw on extra resources to make sure they defeated Dukla Prague 4-1 at White Hart Lane in the return game. Spurs started with a high tempo and were two goals ahead before the quarter-hour mark with Dave Mackay and Bobby Smith calming the home fans' nerves. The same two men grabbed another goal each, with the Czechs only managing a single strike in response.

SATURDAY 26th FEBRUARY 1972

Veteran striker Alan Gilzean keeps up his impressive record of scoring in every FA Cup tie this season to help Tottenham Hotspur progress to the quarter-final stage. The 33-year-old former Dundee and Scotland forward, who spent ten years at White Hart Lane, opens the scoring against Everton before 1966 World Cup-winner Martin Peters completes the scoring at Goodison Park.

SATURDAY 26th FEBRUARY 2011

Former Spurs defender Dean Richards dies aged 36 after suffering from a long-term illness. Richards cost Spurs £8.1m when he arrived from Southampton in 2001, but would only manage 73 appearances for the club in a four-year spell at White Hart Lane. He was the victim of persistent injuries and doctors advised him against continuing his career due to dizzy spells and headaches forcing Richards to retire in 2005.

SATURDAY 27th FEBRUARY 1971

The club's first League Cup Final ends in victory, as Spurs beat Third Division Aston Villa 2-0 at Wembley. The Villains were the better side early on, but the Lilywhites' class eventually shines through as Martin Chivers scores two goals in five minutes to guarantee that the trophy would be heading back to White Hart Lane.

SUNDAY 27th FEBRUARY 1994

Spurs score three goals away to Chelsea, but still lose in a seven-goal thriller at Stamford Bridge in the Premier League. Steve Sedgley, Jason Dozzell and Andy Gray were all on target for Spurs, but it was not enough as goals from John Spencer, two from Mark Stein and another from Mal Donaghy, ensures victory for the Blues.

MONDAY 28th FEBRUARY 1927

Former player Billy Minter is handed the reins at Spurs as he becomes manager. Unfortunately, his tenure was not a successful one, as the team were relegated from the top flight in his first season in charge, and he was unable to take them back to the heights they had recently enjoyed. He retired from his role after 18 months in charge, and took on the less stressful role of assistant club secretary, a position he held until his death in 1940.

WEDNESDAY 28th FEBRUARY 1979

Steve Perryman scores the only goal of the game as Tottenham book their place in the quarter-finals of the FA Cup with a hard-fought fifth-round win over Oldham Athletic. The midfielder, who spent 17 years at Spurs and won the Football Writers' Association Player of the Year in 1982 – amongst various other domestic honours – scored his first goal of the season at Boundary Park to send Keith Burkinshaw's team through to the next round.

WEDNESDAY 28th FEBRUARY 1996

A blizzard had forced the abandonment of the original match against Nottingham Forest, with the players unable to see any more than a yard ahead and the City Ground was blanketed with snow. In better conditions, there was no outright winner again for this re-arranged game as Spurs drew 2-2 with Chris Armstrong bagging a brace for Tottenham.

SATURDAY 29th FEBRUARY 1936

Spurs crash out of the FA Cup at the quarter-final stage at the hands of Sheffield United after losing 3-1. Spurs had beaten Southend United, Huddersfield Town and Bradford Park Avenue to reach this stage of the competition, but the Blades had the cutting edge on the day and dispatched Jack Tresadern's team in clinical style at Bramall Lane. The Yorkshire outfit went on to the final, but were beaten by Arsenal courtesy of a solitary goal from England international Ted Drake. It was a final Spurs fans simply couldn't win!

SATURDAY 29th FEBRUARY 1964

Due to the infrequent nature of this date being used for football fixtures, Spurs have done little of note in leap years. On one of the few occasions the date fell on a match day, Cliff Jones and Jimmy Greaves score the goals that make the difference in a 2-1 win over Birmingham City at St Andrew's to give an understrength Spurs the two points in this First Division fixture. The victory keeps the Lilywhites four points clear at the top of Division One with a game in hand over nearest challengers Blackburn Rovers.

SPURS
On This Day

MARCH

WEDNESDAY 1st MARCH 1995

Israeli forward Ronny Rosenthal's Spurs career is best remembered for his quick-fire hat-trick that turned an FA Cup tie against Southampton on its head. Tottenham found themselves two goals down by half-time, but the moment Gerry Francis brought Rosenthal off the bench, the game changed completely. The former Liverpool star scored twice to take the match to extra time where he completed his hat-trick, before Teddy Sheringham, Nicky Barmby and Darren Anderton rounded off the scoring to give Spurs a breathless 6-2 victory and complete an incredible comeback.

SUNDAY 2nd MARCH 1986

Steve Perryman makes his final league appearance in a 2-1 defeat to Liverpool at White Hart Lane. Overall, Perryman played a record 655 times for Spurs since making his debut in 1969. He captained the team to their 1980s successes and was loved by fans for his on-field leadership skills. Upon being dropped by Spurs, he decided it was time to move on and joined Oxford United.

FRIDAY 3rd MARCH 1972

Darren Anderton is born in Southampton. The midfielder started his career in nearby Portsmouth under the tutelage of Alan Ball before being snapped up by Spurs in 1992 where he would stay for the next 12 years. He was, somewhat unfairly, criticised for his fitness record, earning the nickname 'Sick Note' over a period of time – even though he made almost 300 league appearances for Spurs and also represented England on 30 occasions. Anderton was inducted into the Tottenham Hotspur Hall of Fame in 2009. Away from White Hart Lane he enjoyed spells at Wolverhampton Wanderers and AFC Bournemouth until his retirement from the game in December 2008.

SATURDAY 3rd MARCH 1973

Spurs defeat Norwich City to win the League Cup while also becoming the first club to win the trophy twice. Ralph Coates' strike proves to be the only difference between the two sides in a closely contested game. Coates started the game on the bench, but had to replace the injured John Pratt after only 25 minutes. Norwich were under pressure for large portions of the match, but their resolute defence couldn't hold out all game and Coates struck the winner in the 72nd minute to send one half of Wembley wild.

SATURDAY 4th MARCH 1961

In the historic double-winning season, the FA Cup sixth-round tie against Sunderland almost ended Spurs' dream of re-writing the history books. The game was played at Roker Park, and Spurs looked to have few problems against the Second Division outfit after Cliff Jones put them in the lead in the ninth minute. Sunderland came out stronger after the break, scrambling an equaliser, and could have had more if it wasn't for Tottenham's rearguard action which stood tall to earn a replay at White Hart Lane that Bill Nicholson's side duly romped 5-1.

SUNDAY 4th MARCH 2007

The game of the season as West Ham United and Spurs serve up a derby cracker at Upton Park. Things had looked rosy for the Hammers after Mark Noble put them ahead on 16 minutes and even more so when Carlos Tevez struck a 41st-minute free kick past Paul Robinson to double the Irons' advantage. But a Jermain Defoe penalty reduces arrears six minutes after the break and Teemu Tainio volleyed home the equaliser on 63 minutes to send the travelling Spurs fans wild. West Ham, however, appeared set to take all three points when former Spurs striker Bobby Zamora made it 3-2 with just five minutes remaining – but the best was yet to come. Dimitar Berbatov drew Spurs level in the last minute of normal time and Paul Stalteri prodded home a dramatic winner for the Lilywhites four minutes into time added on to complete a memorable afternoon in the East End.

SATURDAY 5th MARCH 1938

A record attendance of 75,038 witness Spurs lose at White Hart Lane against Sunderland in the FA Cup. It could have been better for Spurs had a seemingly good goal not been controversially disallowed. The linesman deemed that Jack Gibbons had handled the ball into the net but it was a dubious decision and a tough call at best. The opposition go on to score the only goal of the game and progress in the competition.

SATURDAY 6th MARCH 1971

Spurs earn a terrific 0-0 draw at Anfield in the FA Cup sixth round, but fail to make home advantage count in the replay, losing 1-0 to Bill Shankly's Liverpool.

TUESDAY 6th MARCH 1985

Spurs lose their unbeaten home record in European competition as Real Madrid win by a single goal at White Hart Lane in the first leg of a frenetic Uefa Cup quarter-final. The unfortunate Steve Perryman was the man that changed the game as he bundled the ball into his own net after Ray Clemence had saved a shot from the Spanish giants.

SUNDAY 7th MARCH 1993

Nayim is the inspiration as Spurs defeat Manchester City in an FA Cup quarter-final at Maine Road. The 4-2 victory means that they would take on Arsenal in what would become an infamous semi-final. The diminutive Spaniard netted a hat-trick, with Steve Sedgley scoring the other to break City fans' hearts, hopeful of a first Wembley appearance for 12 years. Even more so when Mike Sheron put the Blues ahead – but as Tottenham bounce back and take a 4-1 lead, the home fans invade the pitch in the hope that the game would be abandoned. Order was eventually restored by police, allowing the match to be completed and Terry Phelan scored a late consolation.

WEDNESDAY 8th MARCH 1961

Spurs take on Sunderland in an FA Cup replay with Tottenham hitting five to mark sure they advanced to the next round. It is claimed that fans queued for up to ten hours outside the ground as they dreamt of witnessing Spurs progress to the semi-finals. Those lucky enough to get in were not disappointed as goals from Les Allen, Bobby Smith, Dave Mackay and two from Terry Dyson, confirmed passage to the next round.

MONDAY 9th MARCH 1953

In a second replay against Birmingham City played at Wolverhampton Wanderers' Molineux, Spurs run out eventual winners with Sonny Walters scoring the solitary goal that gave the men in white the victory. The first two games ended in a 1-1 draw at St Andrew's and a 2-2 finish after extra time in the return match in north London. Walters, a talented winger and integral member of the historic double-winning side, made a total of 234 appearances and scored 71 goals – he also bagged Spurs' 1,500th league goal at White Hart Lane just five weeks before his winner against Birmingham City.

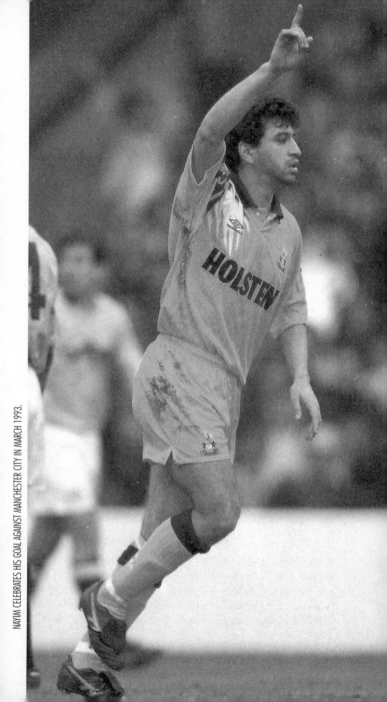

WEDNESDAY 9th MARCH 2011

Spurs keep a clean sheet to ensure further progress in the Champions League knockout phase. The mighty AC Milan were unable to overturn the one-goal deficit from the first leg in the San Siro and with Spurs defending stoutly, the Italians found themselves victims of a classic Italian-style European display by Harry Redknapp's side. Peter Crouch's strike in the first leg proves sufficient as the seven-time European Cup winners crashed out of the competition and Spurs went marching on.

MONDAY 10th MARCH 1919

Arsenal confirmed their place as Spurs' rivals, on and off the pitch; the Gunners had previously moved north from Woolwich to make Tottenham their geographical rivals. However, with the Football League looking to re-start after the end of World War I, Arsenal managed to take Spurs' place in the First Division causing outrage at White Hart Lane, and ultimately forming a bitter rivalry that is as strong today as it was when it first began!

SATURDAY 11th MARCH 1995

Spurs' FA Cup momentum was gathering pace and they went to Anfield confident of progressing at Liverpool's expense. That optimism seemed misplaced as the home side took a one-goal lead before the break, but strikes from Teddy Sheringham and Jurgen Klinsmann were enough to give Spurs the win, and a place in the semi-finals.

TUESDAY 12th MARCH 1912

George 'Willie' Hall is born in Newark, Nottinghamshire. Hall was an impressive inside-forward who began his career in his home county with Notts County, before joining Tottenham for £2,500 in 1932. His most famous moment was undoubtedly when he scored five goals inside 30 minutes for England in a match against Northern Ireland and Hall is still the record holder for the fastest international hat-trick.

TUESDAY 12th MARCH 1957

Bobby Smith's third hat-trick of the campaign is instrumental in Spurs' 4-1 dismantling of Bolton Wanderers. They were Smith's fifth, sixth and seventh goals in three outings, which proved his immense worth to a team on the up. The hosts' scoring on the day was completed by Johnny Brooks with the Lancastrians unable to deal with a rampant Tottenham outfit.

SATURDAY 13th MARCH 1982

One of the more forgettable showpiece occasions for Spurs as they lose the League Cup Final 3-1 to Liverpool in extra time. It was a disappointing result for the club in its centenary year, especially considering it meant they relinquished a unique claim of having never been defeated in a domestic cup final. It could have been much better for the Lilywhites after taking the lead through a Steve Archibald goal. Sadly, it wasn't to be as two goals from Ronnie Whelan, and one from Ian Rush, helped Liverpool retain the trophy in their first League Cup Final since beating Norwich City in 1973.

MONDAY 14th MARCH 1898

Frank Brettell is appointed as the club's first manager. The Liverpudlian had been a key figure in the formation of Everton Football Club in his hometown and he brought a lot of players with him from his former club. Sadly, he was unable to bring success to Tottenham and his period in charge was a short one, leaving the club less than a year later.

WEDNESDAY 14th MARCH 1962

A tactical masterclass from Ipswich Town proves too much for a Spurs side who go into this game still fighting for trophies on all fronts, but leave having lost 3-1. The second-versus-third clash is embarrassingly one-sided at times with Alf Ramsey's team's style and formation causing Bill Nicholson's team continual problems. The only upside for Spurs was a consolation goal from Jimmy Greaves in the 3-1 defeat. Ipswich Town, with 14 wins out of 16 at Portman Road, increase the points gap to five as a result.

SUNDAY 15th MARCH 1987

Spurs travel to south London with the unenviable prospect of having to get past the Crazy Gang – also known as Wimbledon – to gain a place in the FA Cup semi-finals. The players and fans shouldn't have worried as, like on many occasions, the duo of Glenn Hoddle and Chris Waddle were on hand to inspire Spurs to victory, with each bagging a goal in front of the TV cameras to secure a 2-0 win at the claustrophobic surroundings of Plough Lane.

MONDAY 16th MARCH 1970

Club legend Jimmy Greaves, arguably the finest and easily most prolific striker in the history of Tottenham Hotspur, is sold to London rivals West Ham United in a part-exchange deal involving Martin Peters. After 124 goals in 157 starts for Chelsea, he joined AC Milan in 1961 and scored nine goals in 12 games but failed to settle in Italy so Bill Nicholson signed him for Spurs for £99,999. The unusual fee was intended to relieve Greaves of the pressure of being the first £100,000 player and he soon settled in to life at the Lane. His 266 goals for the club, in just 379 appearances, remains a club record and he only once finished a full season with less than 20 goals. A genuine club legend and one of the greatest finishers the world has ever seen.

SATURDAY 16th MARCH 1985

It had been 73 years since Spurs had recorded a victory at Anfield, so it came as something of a shock when a Garth Crooks goal was enough to earn all the points against a fine Liverpool outfit. To make the result slightly more remarkable, it was exactly 73 years to the day since the Lilywhites' last win at the ground.

SATURDAY 17th MARCH 1956

Manchester City defeat Spurs 1-0 in an FA Cup semi-final at Villa Park. The disappointment was exaggerated by the fact it was also Danny Blanchflower's last game as captain for two years, following a falling out with the manager which ultimately led to the Northern Irishman resigning from his position.

SATURDAY 18th MARCH 1961

Another trip to Villa Park for a semi-final in the world's most famous domestic cup competition is a successful one for Spurs. Burnley were the opposition on the day, and were easily defeated as Bobby Smith scores twice, and Cliff Jones nets, in a 3-0 win over the team from Turf Moor.

SATURDAY 18th MARCH 2006

Second-half goals from Aaron Lennon and Robbie Keane give Spurs a 2-0 victory away to Birmingham City. The victory keeps fourth-place Tottenham just ahead of Arsenal in the battle for Champions League football.

FA CUP FINAL
WEMBLEY
1982

SATURDAY 19th MARCH 1966

Spurs share ten goals with Aston Villa at White Hart Lane in a remarkable 90 minutes of rollercoaster football. The score ends 5-5, though the hosts had actually gone 5-1 up at one stage thanks to goals from Alan Gilzean, Jimmy Greaves, Frank Saul, Laurie Brown and Jimmy Robertson. Villa refused to throw in the towel and are rewarded by Tottenham's implosion, earning a share of the spoils.

WEDNESDAY 20th MARCH 1974

Spurs go into the second leg of their Uefa Cup tie against Cologne with a 2-1 lead from the away leg. Martin Chivers, Martin Peters and Ralph Coates all score in the comprehensive 3-0 win over the Germans to confirm Tottenham's passage to the semi-final.

SATURDAY 21st MARCH 1964

Recent acquisition from Fulham, Alan Mullery makes his Spurs debut in a match against Manchester United. The 22-year-old cost the club £72,500 to move across London, but it proves to be money well spent. Mullery was a strong midfielder who exuded confidence on the pitch, making him the first name on any team sheet. During his time at the club he won the FA Cup, League Cup and Uefa Cup, and made 312 league appearances. Mullery returned to Fulham in 1972.

SUNDAY 21st MARCH 1999

A hard-fought League Cup Final against Leicester City was heading to extra time with a ten-man Spurs side in the ascendancy, despite the dismissal of Justin Edinburgh for reacting to a rash Robbie Savage challenge. Then, one last attack before the whistle blows for the end of normal time. Steffen Iversen bursts down the right flank and into the area where his cross is parried by keeper Kasey Keller for Allan Nielsen to dive in and head home the winner to send the Spurs fans into a state of ecstasy, knowing there wasn't enough time left for the Foxes to respond.

SATURDAY 21st MARCH 2009

Luka Modric scores the only goal as Spurs beat Chelsea 1-0 at White Hart Lane. The Croatian's strike on 50 minutes ends Guus Hiddink's 100% record as interim Chelsea boss and while it eases Spurs' relegation fears it puts a massive dent in the visitors' title aspirations.

WEDNESDAY 22nd MARCH 1961

Spurs were heading for the title when lowly Newcastle United arrived at White Hart Lane, with an easy victory expected for the home team. Things went to plan as Spurs were one up at half-time and in full control. In the second period it was a different story, as Danny Blanchflower missed a penalty, which gave the Magpies belief. They equalised on the hour mark, and scored the winner with only ten minutes left.

FRIDAY 23rd MARCH 1894

Arthur Grimsdell is born in Watford and in future years, he will go on to become a Tottenham great. Grimsdell was the club's captain when they clinched the Second Division championship in 1920 and when they won the FA Cup the following year. Overall, he played 418 games for Tottenham over a 17-year period.

SATURDAY 23rd MARCH 1985

An emphatic 5-1 win over Southampton at White Hart Lane comes with Spurs' season gathering great momentum in the latter stages. Five different players scored as Ossie Ardiles, Mark Falco, Glenn Hoddle, Garth Crooks and Garry Brooke all got a goal each in the demolition of the south coast outfit. Sadly, Spurs couldn't continue this vein of form as they lost five out of their next six home games!

SATURDAY 24th MARCH 1934

George Hunt's hat-trick is enough to see off Newcastle on their own patch as Spurs win 3-1. The striker was in great form, notching three hat-tricks in six matches, this being his second. Hunt was prolific throughout his Spurs career netting 138 goals for the club in 198 appearances.

SATURDAY 25th MARCH 1922

Spurs' FA Cup semi-final against Preston North End takes place at Hillsborough, though it's not an enjoyable occasion for the Tottenham faithful. With the score at 1-1, thanks to Jimmy Seed's strike for Spurs, the north London version of the Lilywhites are denied a second. When Bert Bliss' shot rolled towards the net, the referee bizarrely stopped play to deal with an injured Preston player, much to the bemusement of all at the ground. Insult is added to injury soon after as North End scored a winner to take them to the final.

SATURDAY 26th MARCH 1921

England full-back Tommy Clay has an inspired game – but not in his usual outfield position, as he was forced to play the whole match in goal due to injuries to Spurs' goalkeepers. Sunderland fail to breach the Spurs back four and Tottenham record a famous win when Jimmy Seed grabs the only goal of the game. Clay earns an equal amount of acclaim thanks to his clean sheet at the other end.

SATURDAY 27th MARCH 1965

Title-chasing Spurs manage seven goals against bottom-of-the-table Wolverhampton Wanderers, but concede four goals in what turns out be a match to remember. Eddie Clayton, Les Allen, Alan Gilzean (2) and Cliff Jones (3) score the goals and the 7-4 scoreline is made all the more impressive by the fact it was only 1-1 at half-time meaning that nine goals were scored in the second period. Tottenham's home record remains imperious having now won 15 and drawn three of their 18 matches – easily the best in Division One. Yet away from home Spurs had won one, drawn four and lost 13 – hence the 11-point gap to leaders Chelsea.

THURSDAY 28th MARCH 1901

Spurs took on fellow non-leaguers Reading in an FA Cup replay, running out 3-0 victors thanks to two goals from Sandy Brown, and one from David Copeland. Spurs also have two strikes ruled out by the referee as they progress to the semi-final stage.

SATURDAY 28th MARCH 1936

Spurs demolish Southampton at the Lane, winning 8-0. Three goals in the first 20 minutes from Willie Evans, Joe Meek and George Hunt effectively seal the points while Meek and Hunt go on to collect hat-tricks with Evans adding one to his tally.

SATURDAY 29th MARCH 1986

A feisty north London derby ends with Spurs winning 1-0 at White Hart Lane. Gary Stevens scores the winner in the first half with chances at either end. The Gunners play their part in an entertaining spectacle with only the brilliance of Ray Clemence keeping Spurs in the lead. The only surprise of the game was that no more goals were scored.

MONDAY 30th MARCH 1903

Victory over Queens Park Rangers in the London League ensures that Spurs win the title, finishing four points above West Ham United. The triumph was confirmed thanks to goals from David Copeland, Ted Hughes and Chalmers. This was to be the last time Spurs' first team played in this competition as it was used as a reserve league in years to come.

SUNDAY 30th MARCH 2009

Darren Bent gives Spurs a 26th-minute lead at home to relegation-threatened Newcastle United at White Hart Lane, but Kevin Keegan's side stage a remarkable recovery. Nicky Butt levels on the stroke of half-time for the Magpies and Geremi makes it 2-1 after 52. Michael Owen adds a third on 65 and Obafemi Martins makes it 4-1 seven minutes from time. The defeat is greeted with howls of derision from the home fans as another abject campaign draws to a close. The loss also means Newcastle are just four points behind Spurs who occupy 11th spot.

SATURDAY 31st MARCH 1962

Spurs' attempt to retain the FA Cup moves a step closer after they beat Manchester United at Hillsborough in the semi-final. Goals from Jimmy Greaves, Terry Medwin and Cliff Jones book a place in the final with United beaten 3-1 on the day.

SATURDAY 31st MARCH 1979

Spurs lose 1-0 at Middlesbrough, further underlining the club's role as a mid-table side during the 1978/79 campaign. Firmly rooted in tenth spot, the defeat on Teesside sums up a hugely flat campaign for Keith Burkinshaw's men.

SATURDAY 31st MARCH 2001

Tottenham's Jekyll and Hyde season continues with yet another abject display, this time at Highbury in the north London derby. Arsenal triumph 2-0 to continue their title challenge while Spurs wonder what might have been if they were just a little more effective on the road – they took just seven out of a possible 48 points while losing just once in 15 games at White Hart Lane. So poor are the Lilywhites away from home that only basement side Bradford City have a worse record on their travels.

SPURS
On This Day

APRIL

SATURDAY 1st APRIL 1967

There was no time for April Fool's pranks as Spurs took on Liverpool at White Hart Lane. Jimmy Greaves scored twice as Tottenham made it four league wins on the trot and extended an unbeaten run that started way back in mid-January. The visitors managed a consolation goal, but were overpowered by an in-form Spurs outfit.

WEDNESDAY 2nd APRIL 1952

Len Duquemin's goal separates Spurs and Huddersfield Town on the day, but it was scored in a highly controversial manner as an Eddie Baily corner had struck the referee in the box, rebounded to the player, who then crossed it for Duquemin to convert for a last-minute winner. Theoretically, the goal should have been disallowed as Baily had touched the ball twice without another member of either team touching the ball. The goal stood, and Spurs got the points to move within two points of leaders Manchester United.

MONDAY 2nd APRIL 2001

The messiah returns home as Glenn Hoddle is given the task of managing the team he served with such distinction as a player. A gifted midfielder who played more than 450 games, and scored over 100 goals for the Lilywhites during a dozen years at White Hart Lane, is thrown into the deep end with his first game in charge of Spurs – an FA Cup semi-final against local rivals Arsenal! Though he loses that game 2-1, his most memorable moment with the club came when he took his side to the League Cup Final in 2002, though his players picked up losers' medals on the day. The former England manager was removed from his role in September 2003 following a poor start to the campaign, perhaps adding weight to the old saying 'you can never go back'.

SATURDAY 3rd APRIL 1982

Division Two side Leicester City stood in Spurs' way of making it to yet another FA Cup Final. Villa Park hosted the game which saw Argentine midfielder Ossie Ardiles continuously booed due to the conflict taking place in the Falklands. The Foxes started as rank outsiders, but held firm until the 56th minute when Ardiles crossed for Garth Crooks to score. Victory was confirmed when Leicester conceded an own goal late on to make it 2-0 and put Spurs into the final for the second successive season.

MONDAY 4th APRIL 1983

Spurs hosted local rivals Arsenal in a memorable derby at White Hart Lane – for all the right reasons. The Gunners came into the game just one point behind Spurs in the league and the packed crowd expected nothing less than a closely fought game – it proved to be anything but. Spurs annihilated Arsenal in a 5-0 win to claim the bragging rights over the summer months and beyond. Chris Hughton and Mark Falco both netted twice, with Alan Brazil grabbing the other, inflicting one of the most embarrassing derby results in Arsenal's history.

THURSDAY 5th APRIL 1962

Trailing by two goals from the first leg, Spurs had an uphill task when Benfica arrived at White Hart Lane in the European Cup semi-final. Conceding an early away goal didn't help proceedings, but Tottenham laid siege to the Portuguese team's goal for the remainder of the match. Jimmy Greaves had a goal disallowed before Bobby Smith pulled Spurs level on the night. Danny Blanchflower converted a penalty to make it 2-1, but despite a heroic display, Benfica had just done enough to reach the final.

TUESDAY 5th APRIL 2011

Spurs had taken Europe by storm in the first Champions League campaign in the club's history. Having already eliminated both Inter and AC Milan, Real Madrid held no fear for Harry Redknapp's swashbuckling side. Unfortunately, Tottenham saved their worst display for this game, losing 4-0 to Jose Mourinho's side in the Santiago Bernabeu. Peter Crouch was sent off early on – with the team already a goal down there was no way back from there as the Spaniards scored three more, exposing the one-man advantage superbly. With such a mountain to climb, it was unsurprising that Spurs were unable to turn it around in the second leg, but still gave it a go, losing 1-0 on the night.

SATURDAY 6th APRIL 1968

Spurs easily dismantle Southampton 6-1 at White Hart Lane. Alan Mullery starts the scoring with Jimmy Greaves adding two and Martin Chivers and Cliff Jones getting one apiece, before the Saints conceded an own goal, which summed up their day's efforts. This was the club's third straight win in the run-up to Easter.

SATURDAY 7th APRIL 1982

Spurs face Spanish giants Barcelona in the first leg of the European Cup Winners' Cup semi-final at White Hart Lane. The football wasn't of the highest quality as the Catalans seemed intent on mayhem with some brutal challenges that infuriated the home fans. Their approach had the desired result for Barcelona as they earned the draw they had come intent on getting, come what may. Barcelona eventually went ahead, but were pegged back late on when Graham Roberts nodded home a Glenn Hoddle free kick to give Spurs hope going into the second leg.

TUESDAY 8th APRIL 1901

Spurs defeat West Bromwich Albion at Villa Park to book their place in the season's showpiece event at Crystal Palace. The 4-0 FA Cup semi-final win capped off a fantastic run to the final for Tottenham and Sandy Brown was the hero on the day with a remarkable individual display, scoring all four goals for the Lilywhites. It continued his record of netting in every round of the competition.

MONDAY 9th APRIL 1917

William 'Ronnie' Burgess is born in Cwm, Wales. The wing-half had been a miner prior to signing professionally with Spurs when he joined from local side Cwm Villa in 1919. He played for Tottenham for the next 15 years, captaining the team to the 1951 First Division title. Burgess would later manage Watford and the Welsh national side. He died in February, 2005.

SUNDAY 9th APRIL 1995

Elland Road was the destination for Spurs as they hoped to overcome Everton in order to reach the FA Cup Final. Sadly, all did not go to plan as the Toffees ran out 4-1 victors in a largely one-sided affair. A Spurs team ravaged by injury soon fell two behind, but hope was restored when talismanic forward Jurgen Klinsmann converted a penalty. Any lingering thoughts of a comeback were extinguished as Everton scored twice more late on to confirm victory.

SUNDAY 9th APRIL 2000

Liverpool, predictably, beat Spurs at Anfield in their quest to catch leaders Manchester United. The Reds win 2-0 as mid-table Tottenham's mediocre campaign draws to a close.

SATURDAY 9th APRIL 2010

Spurs and Stoke serve up a feast of first-half goals at White Hart Lane. Peter Crouch and Luka Modric put the hosts 2-0 up before Matty Etherington pulls one back. Crouch's second makes it 3-1 but Kenwyne Jones scores just before the break to make it 3-2 – the last goal of the game.

SUNDAY 10th APRIL 2005

Jermain Defoe's 42-minute goal proves enough to give Spurs a 1-0 win over Newcastle United. It's the England striker's 22nd goal of the campaign and lifts Martin Jol's men up into seventh spot.

SATURDAY 11th APRIL 1981

Wolverhampton Wanderers take Spurs to extra time in the FA Cup semi-final at Hillsborough. Spurs lead 2-1 with only a minute to go thanks to goals from Steve Archibald and Glenn Hoddle but it was Hoddle who conceded a last-minute spot kick that was converted by Wolves. The extra 30 minutes couldn't separate the teams and the game ends 2-2. A replay is needed to find the team who will face Manchester City in the Centenary FA Cup Final.

WEDNESDAY 12th APRIL 1967

Second Division Birmingham City are ruthlessly dispatched in an FA Cup sixth-round replay at White Hart Lane, as Spurs score six goals without reply. Terry Venables sets the hosts on their way with two early goals before Alan Gilzean bags another prior to the break. There is no respite for Blues as Jimmy Greaves matches Venables' brace, with Frank Saul completing the scoring on a miserable day for the Midlands outfit.

MONDAY 13th APRIL 1970

The Alan Gilzean and Jimmy Greaves partnership continues to blossom as both are on target in a 2-1 win over Manchester United in the season's penultimate game. The win puts Spurs within a point of Arsenal in the battle to finish north London's top side, though the fact both teams are hopelessly adrift in mid-table takes the shine off the challenge somewhat.

SUNDAY 14th APRIL 1991

Paul Gascoigne returns from injury to inspire Spurs to a 3-1 FA Cup semi-final win over Arsenal at Wembley. Gazza sets the tone early on by smashing home a 35-yard free kick to give his team the lead and Gary Lineker soon doubles the advantage as Tottenham look to complete what was seen as an unlikely victory prior to kick-off, champions-elect Arsenal having lost just once in the league all season. Alan Smith halves the deficit moments before the break but Lineker adds a third on 78 minutes to send half of the 80,000 crowd delirious and confirm Tottenham's place in the 1991 FA Cup Final.

WEDNESDAY 14th APRIL 2010

Danny Rose scores a blistering volley on his Premier League debut as Spurs all-but end Arsenal's title hopes at White Hart Lane. The 19-year-old opens the scoring after just ten minutes and Gareth Bale makes it two just after the start of the second half. Nicklas Bendtner pulls one back but it's too little too late for the Gunners.

WEDNESDAY 15th APRIL 1981

Spurs' FA Cup semi-final replay against Wolves is played across north London at Highbury, giving Keith Burkinshaw's side a slightly unfair advantage – according to Wolves supporters. An early Garth Crooks strike puts Spurs in the box seat and the Black Country outfit are eventually overwhelmed as he adds another. Ricky Villa seals the victory with a screamer from 30 yards to complete the win, and send the team to Wembley to face Manchester City.

SATURDAY 15th APRIL 2006

A Robbie Keane strike on 33 minutes is enough to give Spurs an impressive 1-0 win away to Everton to move on to 61 points – four clear of Arsenal in fifth.

MONDAY 16th APRIL 1900

Spurs become Southern League champions for the only time in their non-league history as they defeat Sheppey United 3-0. Hyde, Pratt and Kirwan were the men that confirmed the title for Spurs that day with a game to spare. It was a stepping stone for the side as they would go on to bigger and better things the following season.

ONE OF THE GREATEST EVER WEMBLEY GOALS: PAUL GASCOIGNE FIRES HIS FAMOUS FREE KICK AGAINST ARSENAL IN APRIL 1991.

MONDAY 17th APRIL 1922

With three games still left to play, Liverpool boss David Ashworth guides his side to a 2-1 victory over Burnley to ensure the Reds are crowned champions of England for the third time. Ashworth is aided by his former club Oldham Athletic, who beat second-place Spurs 1-0 at Boundary Park, giving Liverpool an unassailable lead at the top of Division One.

MONDAY 17th APRIL 1961

The title is leaders Spurs' to lose as nearest challengers Sheffield Wednesday visit White Hart Lane. A win will guarantee Tottenham, six points clear with four games to go, the title. Understandably, both teams look tense and nervous early on with so much at stake. Wednesday struck first on the half-hour mark, but the prolific Bobby Smith got Spurs back on level terms just before half-time. Les Allen made it 2-1 shortly after, which completed the scoring for the game. The victory was enough to crown Spurs champions with fans celebrating long into the night following the Lilywhites' second league championship in a decade.

SATURDAY 18th APRIL 1998

A six-pointer at Oakwell where Spurs take on Barnsley with Premier League safety at stake. Both teams were battling relegation with a win for the visitors taking them above Tottenham and out of the bottom three. Christian Gross' side fall behind on 19 minutes, but Colin Calderwood saves the day with an equaliser in the second half in the tense battle in South Yorkshire. Swiss defender Ramon Vega is sent off with 25 minutes left on the clock, but Spurs manage to hold on for a precious point.

WEDNESDAY 19th APRIL 1972

Spurs reach their second European final by disposing of AC Milan in the Uefa Cup after an unforgettable evening at White Hart Lane. Tottenham had won 2-1 in the San Siro, giving them the advantage as the teams entered the second leg and Alan Mullery settles the home fans' nerves by scoring in the first half. AC Milan's pressure finally fashions an equaliser, but the Italians can't find a second and the hosts hang on to win 3-2 on aggregate, much to the delight of a packed White Hart Lane.

SATURDAY 20th APRIL 1901

Spurs make it to the FA Cup Final for the first time when they play at the Crystal Palace against Sheffield United. As non-leaguers, Spurs were seen as massive underdogs against the more experienced men from South Yorkshire. A world record crowd of 114,815 people attended the match, which attracted huge interest around the country. United soon took the lead, but the impressive Sandy Brown quickly scored twice to turn it around, before the Yorkshire side equalised to force a replay. So near, yet so far!

WEDNESDAY 20th APRIL 2011

One of the greatest north London derbies of all time does little for either side as Arsenal lose further ground in the title race and Spurs miss the chance to draw level on points with fourth-place Manchester City. The breathless encounter at White Hart Lane begins when Theo Walcott puts the Gunners 1-0 up after five minutes, but Rafael van der Vaart levels within two minutes. Samir Nasri scores again for Arsenal on 12 minutes and the points look to be heading back to the Emirates Stadium on 40 minutes when Robin van Persie makes it 3-1 five minutes before the break – but this breathless encounter is far from over. Tom Huddlestone pulls one back just before the break and Van der Vaart makes it 3-3 from the penalty spot on 70 to set up a grandstand finish that neither side manages to score in.

THURSDAY 21st APRIL 1923

Jimmy Cantrell becomes the oldest player to represent the club when he lines up against Birmingham City, a record he would hold for the next 88 years. At 39 years and 350 days, he played over 150 games for the club and the popular striker was also part of the 1921 FA Cup-winning side.

WEDNESDAY 21st APRIL 1982

Barcelona beat Spurs 1-0 at the Camp Nou. The Catalans were as vicious as they were in the first leg, with Danish superstar Allan Simonsen settling the tie in the second half. Spurs fought valiantly for the entire 90 minutes, but were unable to find a goal of their own to force extra time and the Spaniards triumphed 2-1 on aggregate as a result.

MONDAY 22nd APRIL 1907

Fred Kirkham is appointed Spurs' manager. He was a strange choice for the role, as Kirkham's only previous involvement in football was as one of the country's top referees. Having never played the game to a decent level, he never had a great rapport with the players and became deeply unpopular in the dressing room in what was an incredibly unsuccessful spell in charge. Kirkham left his role after one year with the club, giving himself the red card before anyone else did!

SATURDAY 22nd APRIL 1978

Spurs' promotion hopes stutter when Sunderland visit White Hart Lane. Despite winger Peter Taylor striking within 30 seconds, Sunderland score three unanswered goals to take a 3-1 lead and John Duncan's late second proves little more than a consolation.

SATURDAY 23rd APRIL 1921

Stamford Bridge hosts the FA Cup Final replay between Spurs and Wolves and Jimmy Dimmock is the hero on the day as he fires home on 55 minutes to give Spurs the lead. That was enough on the day as the Lilywhites collect another piece of silverware and enhance their reputation as a cup team yet further.

WEDNESDAY 24th APRIL 1963

Spurs travel to Belgrade in the European Cup Winners' Cup semi-final first leg. John White sets Tottenham on their way with a volley in the first half, but the joy doesn't last long as Belgrade equalise within ten minutes. Terry Dyson put Spurs back in front in the second half to give his team a massive advantage going into the second leg.

MONDAY 25th APRIL 1984

Tottenham's away goal in the Uefa Cup semi-final, first leg proves crucial as the teams reconvene at White Hart Lane. Losing 2-1 from the first match, Micky Hazard scores a free kick after only six minutes, giving the home side 84 minutes to protect their precious lead. The score will be enough to take Spurs to the final and despite intense pressure from Split in the latter stages of a nerve-wracking encounter, Hazard's goal proves enough to send Tottenham through to yet another major cup competition final.

PETER TAYLOR WAS ON TARGET AT SUNDERLAND IN APRIL 1978.

TUESDAY 26th APRIL 1978

Spurs defeat Hull City by a single goal to keep their Second Division promotion campaign on track. It wasn't a simple victory, as bottom-of-the-table Hull keep Spurs at bay for 80 minutes thanks to a mixture of heroic goalkeeping and last-ditch defending. With ten minutes to go, inspirational captain Steve Perryman bagged the winner.

SATURDAY 26th APRIL 2008

Spurs agree to sign Croatian playmaker Luka Modric from Dinamo Zagreb for £15.8m. The midfielder struggled early on in his career in England, which was aided by the fact he was playing in a struggling team. As the team rose to prominence, so did the diminutive Modric, as he played a key role in the club's Champions League qualification, and their subsequent progression in the competition. His passing ability has seen him rightly recognised as one of the finest in his position in Europe. In 2011, he was the subject of a £40m bid from Chelsea, which the Lilywhites rejected out of hand.

SATURDAY 27th APRIL 1901

Spurs win the FA Cup at the second time of asking when they beat Sheffield United 3-1 in a replay at Burnden Park, Bolton. The Blades take the lead early on, but are pegged back by John Cameron in the second period, before Tom Smith and Sandy Brown put Tottenham comfortably ahead. The Blades can't find a way back into the game meaning Spurs have their first major honour.

SATURDAY 27th APRIL 1921

Spurs lift the FA Cup for the second time when Jimmy Dimmock hits the winning goal against Wolves at Stamford Bridge. A crowd of almost 73,000 watch the game, played in damp conditions on a sodden, muddy pitch, but the only goal of the game was worth waiting for as two Berts – Smith and Bliss – combined to send Dimmock through on goal and after holding off a last-ditch defender's challenge, the Tottenham left-winger tucked the ball home to the delight of the majority of the crowd. Dimmock would stay with Spurs until 1930, by which time he'd clocked up 400 games and scored 100 goals.

FRIDAY 27th APRIL 1945

Martin Chivers is born in Southampton. 'Big Chiv' begins his career with his local side Southampton and plays with distinction at The Dell for six years. Chivers grabbed the nation's attention with 96 goals in 175 games, earning him a move to Tottenham. A fee of £125,000 was paid for his services, and he scored on his debut against Sheffield Wednesday. Another 117 league goals followed as he was at the forefront of Spurs' successes in the following years.

SATURDAY 28th APRIL 1951

It is a first league championship for Spurs as they defeat Sheffield Wednesday 1-0 at White Hart Lane. Len Duquemin scores the title clincher for Arthur Rowe's 'push and run' side, which was made all the more impressive by the fact they had only been promoted to the top flight the previous campaign. Ironically, almost ten years to the day later, Tottenham will again clinch the title – against Sheffield Wednesday!

MONDAY 28th APRIL 1975

Desperate to preserve their top-flight status, Spurs take on reigning champions and European Cup finalists Leeds United at White Hart Lane. Cyril Knowles fires home a free kick before five minutes are even on the clock and in an epic performance, Martin Chivers scores in the second half to double Tottenham's lead. Knowles then converts a spot-kick to put the Lilywhites 3-0 up before Leeds pull a goal back. Any hopes of a comeback are ended when Alfie Conn hits a fourth to guarantee the points, even though the Yorkshire side net a second to make the result 4-2. A memorable day for Spurs.

SATURDAY 29th APRIL 1978

Both Spurs and Southampton only need a point each to ensure promotion when they meet at The Dell. Neither side are willing to risk going for the kill with so much at stake and a predictable 90 minutes ensues. Each side got what they wanted as the match ended goalless, with Saints having the better of the game without being able to turn possession into goals. Spurs finish third in the league and are promoted thanks to their superior goal difference, though nobody rushed out to buy a commemorative video of this non-event.

TUESDAY 29th APRIL 1969

Beaten FA Cup finalists Leicester City beat Spurs 1-0 as their battle to avoid relegation receives a much-needed boost. With three games in hand over most of the sides around them, the Foxes needed to win this fixture to have any chance of survival.

SATURDAY 30th APRIL 1910

Going into the final day of the season, it was winner-take-all between Spurs and Chelsea with the victors surviving relegation from the First Division, and the loser relegated. Spurs were the better side on the day and cheered on by 35,000 spectators, Billy Minter and Percy Humphreys scored the goals that gave Tottenham a 2-1 win, condemning Chelsea to the drop.

SATURDAY 30th APRIL 1966

Spurs' hopes of a top-five finish end with a 1-0 defeat at Turf Moor as second-place Burnley triumph 1-0. In what has been a largely mediocre campaign, Tottenham fans at least take solace that Arsenal's relegation battle will go to the last match of the season having lost 3-0 at Aston Villa on the same day.

SATURDAY 30th APRIL 1981

Wolves take a massive step towards safety with a nervy 1-0 win over Spurs at Molineux. Keith Burkinshaw's side can't finish any higher than ninth with one game remaining. For Wolves, it means leaping out of the bottom three and once again becoming masters of their own destiny – it's also revenge for the FA Cup semi-final defeat to Tottenham, who have Manchester City waiting in the final in what the Lilywhites hope will be a fantastic finish to the 1980/81 campaign.

SUNDAY 30th APRIL 2006

Aaron Lennon scores after 60 minutes to give Spurs a 1-0 win over Bolton Wanderers at White Hart Lane. In a tough, uncompromising match, the Trotters attempt to disrupt Martin Jol's side with stern challenges and direct football – staples of Bolton boss Sam Allardyce's career in football, some might say – but Spurs hold on to claim three valuable points that extends the lead over Arsenal in fifth to seven in the battle for Champions League qualification.

SPURS
On This Day

MAY

WEDNESDAY 1st MAY 1963

Spurs reach their first European final as they beat OFK Belgrade in the second leg of their Uefa Cup tie. Spurs were going to have to do it without the suspended talisman Jimmy Greaves, but even without their prolific marksman, the Lilywhites took the lead through Dave Mackay, before being pegged back by Belgrade. However, Cliff Jones and Bobby Smith restored the advantage as they ran out 3-1 winners to confirm their progression.

SATURDAY 1st MAY 1999

Steve McManaman scores his last goal for Liverpool in a 3-2 victory over Tottenham Hotspur at Anfield before joining Real Madrid for £6m. It's a fitting end to Macca's career at Anfield with his goal proving to be the winner in a game Spurs played a full part in.

SATURDAY 2nd MAY 1998

With relegation from the Premiership a real threat, Spurs travel to Selhurst Park for a match against Wimbledon. Christian Gross' side had been struggling for much of the campaign and his managerial style was continuously coming under question as results repeatedly went against his team. Les Ferdinand put Spurs ahead, but then the visitors concede twice to go behind against a notoriously gritty Dons outfit. But, when a hero was required, up steps Jurgen Klinsmann to score four goals, before setting up Moussa Saib for the sixth to complete an emphatic 6-2 rout and ease fears of the drop. Gross' side now need just a point to guarantee safety in the final match of the season…

WEDNESDAY 3rd MAY 1972

After a difficult campaign, taking on teams from all over Europe, Spurs face Wolverhampton Wanderers in a two-legged Uefa Cup Final. The all-English affair was tentatively played out with both teams eager not to make the mistake that could prove pivotal to the outcome. As it happens, it is Spurs who strike first as Martin Chivers makes it 1-0. Wolves soon equalise thanks to some sloppy defending, but Chivers rifles home a rocket shot from 30 yards to give Spurs a vital first-leg lead.

WEDNESDAY 4th MAY 1949

Arthur Rowe is appointed as the club's new manager. A local boy, having been brought up in Tottenham and a supporter from a young age, Rowe played for Spurs in the 1930s, and was also a full England international in that period. As a manager he was incredibly successful, winning the Second Division in his first full season in charge, using his famous 'push and run' style. Following promotion, he took the team to the First Division, which confirmed his status as a club legend. He resigned from his position in 1956, taking over at Crystal Palace four years later. Rowe died in 1993, but his legacy is still evident in Spurs' playing style to this day.

SATURDAY 4th MAY 1963

Jimmy Greaves sets a new record for the most league goals in a single season by a Spurs player when he scores the third goal in a 4-2 win over Sheffield United – his 37th goal of the campaign. Frank Saul, Cliff Jones and Terry Dyson net a goal each to complete the scoring for the day, but it was Greaves who hit the headlines the following day.

SATURDAY 5th MAY 1962

Spurs take on Burnley at Wembley in the FA Cup Final and it was to be a happy day for the Lilywhites. The Clarets were favourites coming into the game having just finished second in the First Division. However, it didn't go to plan for the Lancastrians as Jimmy Greaves scores early and even after Burnley equalise there was no stopping Spurs as Bobby Smith and Danny Blanchflower net once each as Tottenham retained the FA Cup during a glorious era for the club.

WEDNESDAY 5th MAY 2010

Harry Redknapp completes a remarkable 18 months as Spurs boss as he guides his team into the Champions League for the first time in its present format. Redknapp, who took over Tottenham when the club was bottom of the Premier League, knew that a win at Manchester City would end the Blues' hopes of finishing fourth and guarantee the Lilywhites a Champions League spot. Peter Crouch's late winner caps off a fantastic night and incredible season.

WEDNESDAY 6th MAY 1953

Graeme Souness is born in Edinburgh. One of Scotland's greatest servants, Graeme Souness prowled the midfield for his country for a dozen years and of the 54 caps he won during that time, exactly half were as captain. He began his career with Spurs as an apprentice under Bill Nicholson, signing professional forms as a 15-year-old in 1968. Unable to get a break into the senior team, Souness is said to have told Nicholson that he was the best player at the club! He made one solitary appearance for Spurs in the Uefa Cup as a substitute and after a summer spent with NASL side Montreal Olympique, he returned to England and joined Middlesbrough for £30,000. He later joined Liverpool where he proved his belief in himself to be accurate as he became one of the best players in Europe. One can only wonder what might have been had Spurs given the cocky youngster a run in the team.

SATURDAY 6th MAY 1961

Spurs complete 'the impossible dream' as the Lilywhites follow up the league title with the FA Cup to become the first side in the 20th century to complete the fabled 'double'. Leicester City are all that stand between Spurs and immortality with the FA Cup Final at Wembley. It was a nervous encounter as the pressure seemed to get to both sides and it wasn't until the 69th minute when Bill Nicholson's men finally broke the deadlock, thanks to a superb solo effort from Bobby Smith. It would be the same man that set up the clincher for Terry Dyson who headed home Smith's cross to make it 2-0 and guarantee a second piece of silverware for White Hart Lane's trophy cabinet.

SATURDAY 6th MAY 1967

Tottenham's hopes of finishing runners-up in Division One gets a boost with a hard-fought 0-0 draw at Anfield. With Bill Shankly's Liverpool also harbouring hopes of catching second-place Nottingham Forest, this draw confirms third is the highest the Reds can finish. As it transpires, Spurs beat Sheffield United on the final day to finish level on points with Forest, but with an inferior goal average.

SATURDAY 7th MAY 1977

Spurs have enjoyed their fair share of highs, but this was one of their lowest days as they were mauled 5-0 by Manchester City, all-but confirming relegation from the top flight for the first time in 27 years. City, who still had a shot at winning the Division One title, were in awesome form and the pick of the goals was Peter Barnes' delightful chip over Pat Jennings.

TUESDAY 8th MAY 1979

An uneventful season of mid-table mediocrity comes to an end with Spurs giving prolific youngster Mark Falco his first-team debut in a somewhat meaningless game against Bolton Wanderers at Burnden Park. Falco scores on his debut in a 3-1 win and went on to have a successful career with Spurs, playing a pivotal role in the team of the 1980s. Falco was twice top scorer and was a firm fans' favourite for his hard work ethic.

SATURDAY 9th MAY 1981

The world was watching when Spurs faced Manchester City in the 100th FA Cup Final at Wembley Stadium. While it wasn't a classic, it was an entertaining game nonetheless with Tottenham indebted to City's Tommy Hutchison. It was the tall Scottish winger who headed the Blues ahead in the first half and for so long it looked as though that would be enough to settle the game, but after eavesdropping on a Glenn Hoddle free kick, he managed to peel off the wall and deflect Hoddle's shot past Joe Corrigan to make it 1-1 and earn Spurs a replay. The only other talking point was when the charismatic Ricky Villa walked down the cinder track back to the changing rooms, disgusted at having been substituted.

SUNDAY 10th MAY 1998

Jurgen Klinsmann's final game in his second spell at Spurs was in the final game of the 1997/98 season. Having helped his team guarantee survival for another season, the German scores his side's equaliser in a 1-1 draw at White Hart Lane. It would also be the last time that Gary Mabbutt would be seen in a Tottenham shirt after many fine years of service as the club's captain.

MONDAY 10th MAY 2011

It was the night when Manchester City could confirm their qualification for next season's Champions League with a victory over Spurs, the team who had denied Mancini's men exactly the same prize 12 months earlier. That day, Peter Crouch's goal had settled the match to hand Harry Redknapp's side victory and a bizarre twist of fate would see exactly the same player score the winning goal again – but this time as he put through his own net! It was the perfect fillip for City ahead of the FA Cup Final just four days later but a cruel joke on both Crouch and Spurs.

TUESDAY 11th MAY 1993

Spurs travel to Highbury hopeful of taking all three points with Arsenal putting out a weakened team in anticipation of the FA Cup Final the following week and things panned out exactly as the Tottenham fans had hoped, winning 3-1 with Teddy Sheringham scoring the first, before the relatively unknown John Hendry added two more. The Scottish forward would only play 17 times for the club, with this his most memorable moment in a Spurs shirt. The victory takes the Lilywhites up to eighth in the table, above Arsenal in tenth and level on points with sixth-place Liverpool. All in all, a good end to the campaign.

THURSDAY 12th MAY 1994

Spurs are charged by the Football Association for making illegal payments to players over a four-year period. The problems began when Terry Venables had a disagreement with owner Alan Sugar, who then uttered the immortal lines "Terry, you're fired!" which in turn started an investigation into the club's financial activities. A court case involving the two men cast a cloud over the club for a number of years.

SATURDAY 13th MAY 1967

A third-place finish for Spurs is confirmed with a 2-0 victory over Sheffield United at White Hart Lane. The Tottenham faithful hadn't seen their side lose since January and Jimmy Greaves and Frank Saul were the men that seal a fine result to cap off a fantastic season.

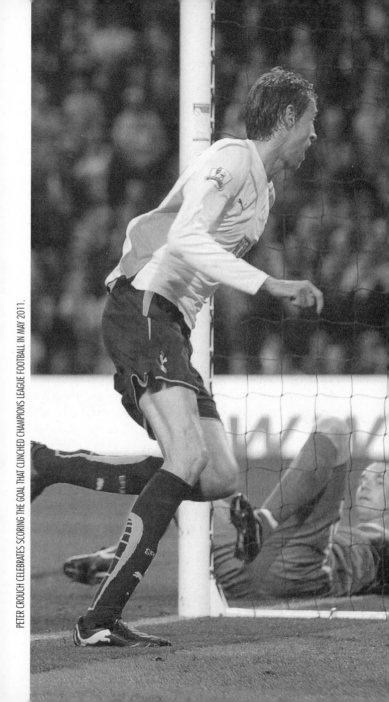

THURSDAY 14th MAY 1981

Spurs are involved in one of the most dramatic and memorable FA Cup finals in history, as they come out on top against Manchester City in the Centenary Cup Final replay. It was end-to-end stuff, with both teams going at each other hammer and tongs in a pulsating encounter. Ricky Villa – who many felt was lucky to keep his place in the side after his sulky behaviour in the first game – scored after just eight minutes, but City soon equalised through a spectacular volley from 30 yards by Steve Mackenzie. The Blues then took the lead in the second period through a Kevin Reeves penalty, but Spurs would not be stopped with Garth Crooks making it 2-2 on 70 minutes. The stage was set for a great finish, and Villa didn't disappoint, as he scored a mesmeric winner by dribbling through City, and calmly slotting past the keeper with 76 minutes on the clock.

WEDNESDAY 15th MAY 1963

Beating Atletico Madrid in the European Cup Winners' Cup Final in Rotterdam should have been a difficult proposition for Spurs, but the reality was far different as the Lilywhites ran out 5-1 victors. Jimmy Greaves and John White set Spurs on their way against the Spaniards. Atletico scored a penalty to make it 2-1 before Terry Dyson restored Tottenham's two-goal lead. Greaves and Dyson then added a goal each to make sure that Spurs were the first British club to lift a European trophy – a magnificent achievement for a club who have achieved many notable firsts.

SATURDAY 15th MAY 1982

Following the introduction of three points for a win, Liverpool win the Division One title for the third time in four seasons after beating Spurs 3-1 at Anfield. Second-place Ipswich Town could have made the season go down to the final game, but they lost 3-1 at home to Nottingham Forest, meaning Liverpool went six points clear at the top of the table with one game to go, ensuring a fifth league title for Bob Paisley. It wasn't exactly the way Spurs wanted to add another entry into the record books!

SATURDAY 16th MAY 1987

Tottenham lose 3-2 to Coventry City in the 1987 FA Cup Final. Things started brightly with Clive Allen notching his 49th of the season but the Sky Blues equalise before Mabbutt restores the lead soon afterwards. Spurs couldn't hold on to the lead with Coventry scoring again to force the fateful extra period in which Gary Mabbutt puts through his own goal to decide the match.

WEDNESDAY 17th MAY 1972

Spurs win the Uefa Cup as a long, tiring season comes to a successful close. Tottenham led Wolves 2-1 from the first leg at Molineux and the advantage was quickly increased when Alan Mullery put Spurs a goal ahead on the night. Wolves levelled before the break but couldn't find the second goal that would have forced extra time. This was Spurs' second European success – another first for a British club.

SATURDAY 18th MAY 1991

Terry Venables' Spurs beat Brian Clough's Nottingham Forest at Wembley in a thrilling FA Cup Final that also sees a wound-up Paul Gascoigne stretchered off after lunging into a challenge. To make things worse, the subsequent free kick was despatched by Stuart Pearce to give Forest the lead, but the match was far from over. Spurs rallied with Gary Lineker having a goal disallowed before Paul Stewart scores a legitimate goal that forces extra-time. On this occasion, an own goal would work in Spurs' favour as Des Walker diverts the ball into his own net to give Tottenham the trophy.

SUNDAY 19th MAY 1957

Long before marketing-orientated pre-season tours to America, teams did travel across the pond just to play football matches. Spurs took on Celtic in New York at the end of the campaign in a showpiece friendly that proves a high-scoring affair. The Bhoys score twice early on, but Bobby Smith pulls one back before Celtic make it 3-1. Spurs recover well and Smith claims two more to complete his hat-trick and make the score 3-3 before Micky Dulin grabs the winner to the delight of the expats in the sizeable Big Apple crowd.

SATURDAY 20th MAY 1961

Clive Allen is born in Stepney. The forward played for a variety of teams around London, before joining Spurs in 1984. On May 20th, 1961, his father Les was a member of the legendary Tottenham Hotspur team that won the First Division title and FA Cup double and his dad helped secure the FA Cup triumph exactly two weeks before Clive was born. Part of a rich football dynasty, Clive is the brother of Bradley Allen and cousin of both Martin Allen and ex-West Ham United and Spurs midfielder Paul Allen. He began his career with QPR, then joined Arsenal for just 62 days during the close season, never kicked a ball and was then off to Crystal Palace in a player-exchange deal with Kenny Sansom! He later returned to Loftus Road to further enhance his reputation. But, it was with Tottenham that he became something of a household name as a lethal goal poacher, very much in the same mould of another Spurs legend, Jimmy Greaves, who, hardly surprisingly, was Allen's idol. Indeed, Greaves enjoyed some of his best years at White Hart Lane, but was immensely proud that it was Allen who broke his record with a spectacular haul of 49 goals in the 1986/87 season. As a result, he collected the PFA Player of the Year and the coveted Football Writers' Association Player of the Year awards that same season. Today he is a member of Harry Redknapp's backroom staff at White Hart Lane.

SATURDAY 20th MAY 1967

Chelsea are the opponents for the 1967 FA Cup Final which sees another Wembley success for Spurs. In the first all-London final, the Tottenham defence copes admirably with Chelsea's attacking flair. Joe Kinnear is the stand-out performer which is all the more impressive by the fact he had only come into the team due to injury to a team-mate. Jimmy Robertson and Frank Saul scored the goals that won the game for the Lilywhites, though Chelsea manage a late consolation through Tambling, but with only five minutes remaining, the Blues ran out of time in their efforts to force a replay.

MONDAY 20th MAY 1991

Spurs take a rare point from Old Trafford after holding Manchester United to a 1-1 draw.

TUESDAY 21st MAY 1974

Spurs take on Dutch Eredivisie side Feyenoord in the Lilywhites' third European final. The first leg of the Uefa Cup Final was played at White Hart Lane with honours even after a hard-fought 2-2 draw. Spurs twice take the lead, but fight back to take an advantage going into the second leg. A Mike England header and an own goal were Spurs' scorers but the odds of success were now stacked against them.

SATURDAY 22nd MAY 1982

Spurs face Second Division Queens Park Rangers in the FA Cup Final. Future Tottenham manager, Terry Venables, was in charge of the Hoops who were determined to deny Spurs in their centenary year. Normal time ended goalless, with neither team able to break down the other's defence. Glenn Hoddle eventually broke the deadlock in extra time, only for Spurs to concede an equaliser which sent the game to a replay.

SUNDAY 22nd MAY 2011

Roman Pavlyuchenko scores three minutes into injury time to give Spurs a 2-1 win over Birmingham City – and confirms Blues' relegation. The same player had given Tottenham a 49th-minute lead before Craig Gardner levels ten minutes from time and, at that point, a draw would have been good enough.

WEDNESDAY 23rd MAY 1984

Tottenham and Anderlecht can't be separated after the second leg of the Uefa Cup Final ends just as it had in Belgium – in a 1-1 draw. Stand-in skipper Graham Roberts scores Spurs' equaliser with only six minutes left on the clock to take the game to extra time. The additional period saw no further scoring meaning a penalty shoot-out was needed to settle the match. Spurs were without first-choice custodian Ray Clemence, which brought a new hero to the fore as his deputy Tony Parks becomes a club legend in the space of ten minutes. With Spurs leading 4-3, Parks saves Anderlecht's fifth penalty to win the trophy before setting on a mammoth run around the White Hart Lane pitch to celebrate – a nice way for outgoing manager Keith Burkinshaw to end his reign as Tottenham boss.

SUNDAY 24th MAY 1914

An ill-advised end-of-season trip to Germany gave the Spurs players a change of scenery, though the games were played against the backdrop of imminent war between the British and the Germans. This caused the genial hosts to make some brutal challenges during the games as Spurs were caught in the middle of a political nightmare. On this particular day, Spurs drew 1-1 with Stuttgart but the players came off the worse for wear with several nursing nasty knocks and bruises. So bad was the Lilywhites' treatment that chairman Charles Roberts declared: "No Spurs team will ever again visit Germany while I am still alive." He was true to his word and Tottenham didn't return to Germany until 1950, some seven years after Roberts' death.

TUESDAY 25th MAY 1994

A worrying day for Spurs fans when the FA announce their contingency plans if they decide to forcibly demote the club to the Second Division – if they are found guilty with regards to illegal player payments. The FA claim that recently-relegated Sheffield United would be allowed to maintain their top-flight status if Spurs are punished. Fortunately, the FA decided not to take such drastic action.

FRIDAY 25th MAY 2007

Spurs strike a deal with Southampton to sign wonder kid Gareth Bale. The 17-year-old Welshman had taken the Championship by storm and attracted the attention of a host of top teams, most notably Manchester United, but it is Spurs who get Bale's signature. Since then, Bale has become an integral part of the Spurs line-up with some classic wing play – none better than his hat-trick against Inter Milan at the San Siro in 2010 – which sees him win the PFA Players' Player of the Year in 2011.

SATURDAY 26th MAY 1962

Spurs visit Israel for a two-game tour. The club took on a Tel Aviv XI as part of the trip with a full-strength squad travelling. In this game they manage a 2-2 draw thanks to Dave Mackay and Eddie Clayton bagging a goal each.

THURSDAY 27th MAY 1982

Wembley was becoming almost a second home to Spurs as they faced QPR in the FA Cup Final replay and this time the Lilywhites came out on top. Graham Roberts is fouled in the area, giving Glenn Hoddle the opportunity to put his team in front – and he gladly took it. Rangers didn't lie down, and came back at Spurs in the hope of finding an equaliser, but Ray Clemence was in top form and managed to keep out everything the Hoops could throw at him. The victory meant that Tottenham had now won all seven of the FA Cup finals that they had taken part in – quite a record!

WEDNESDAY 28th MAY 1952

Spurs manage to hit an incredible 18 when they faced a Saskatchewan FA XI on an end-of-season tour of the USA. Spurs had 14 by the time the half-time whistle had blown, which then saw a strange event – that could only happen in a friendly – the two sides swap goalkeepers!

WEDNESDAY 29th MAY 1974

Spurs face an uphill battle as they tried to defeat Feyenoord in Holland in the second leg of the Uefa Cup Final. On the night, Spurs lose 2-0 to go down 4-2 overall on aggregate but it's events off the pitch that grab the headlines as riots start in the stands between rivals fans. Bill Nicholson tries to calm the fans down but his words have little effect.

SATURDAY 30th MAY 1970

A casual three-match tour or Switzerland was the players' reward for winning the FA Cup. They faced FC Zurich in the opening game, winning 2-0 thanks to a brace from Jimmy Robertson. Other opposition on the tour was BSC Young Boys and FC Servette, with Spurs recording victories in those matches before setting off on their deserved summer break.

FRIDAY 31st MAY 1963

Spurs travel to South Africa for a close-season tour. A representative XI selected by the national football association were easily defeated 5-1, but the game will be remembered for the career-ending leg-break suffered by Welsh winger, Terry Medwin.

SPURS
On This Day

JUNE

MONDAY 1st JUNE 1959

The USSR play host to Spurs on an end-of-season tour, with their most important game coming against Dynamo Kiev. Spurs win the game 2-1, with Johnny Brookes bagging a brace. These friendlies were seen as a turning point for a great Spurs side in the making, with onlookers believing that the players acquired were gelling and understanding how manager Bill Nicholson wanted them to play.

SATURDAY 2nd JUNE 1951

Four hundred people attend a celebratory dinner at The Savoy in acknowledgement of Spurs' first championship title. All players and club officials were there, with many giving speeches in praise of the club's achievement with particular reference to Arthur Rowe's pivotal role in the success. Appreciation was also shown to the loyal supporters who had played their part in the historic season, by the players and club officials.

FRIDAY 3rd JUNE 2011

Goalkeeper Brad Friedel signs on a free transfer from Aston Villa. The experienced American made the Bosman switch after making over 400 appearances in the Premier League. The 40-year-old has also played for Liverpool and Blackburn Rovers in the English top flight, and was brought in to add competition for the number-one spot. His home Premier League debut against Everton is postponed due to the Tottenham riots and Friedel instead makes his bow in a 5-0 Europa League victory to Hearts before making his league debut in a 3-0 defeat to Manchester United at Old Trafford. Despite keeping a clean sheet on his home debut against Hearts in a 0-0 draw, it was followed by a 5-1 defeat to Manchester City on his league home debut.

SUNDAY 4th JUNE 1966

A lengthy end-of-season tour around North and Central America continues. The Lilywhites' schedule includes an exhausting eleven matches against the likes of Glasgow Celtic, who they played on this day, and a plethora of little-known American sides. Terry Venables had previously only played once for the club, but scored the winner as Spurs beat the Scots by a single goal in a match played in New York.

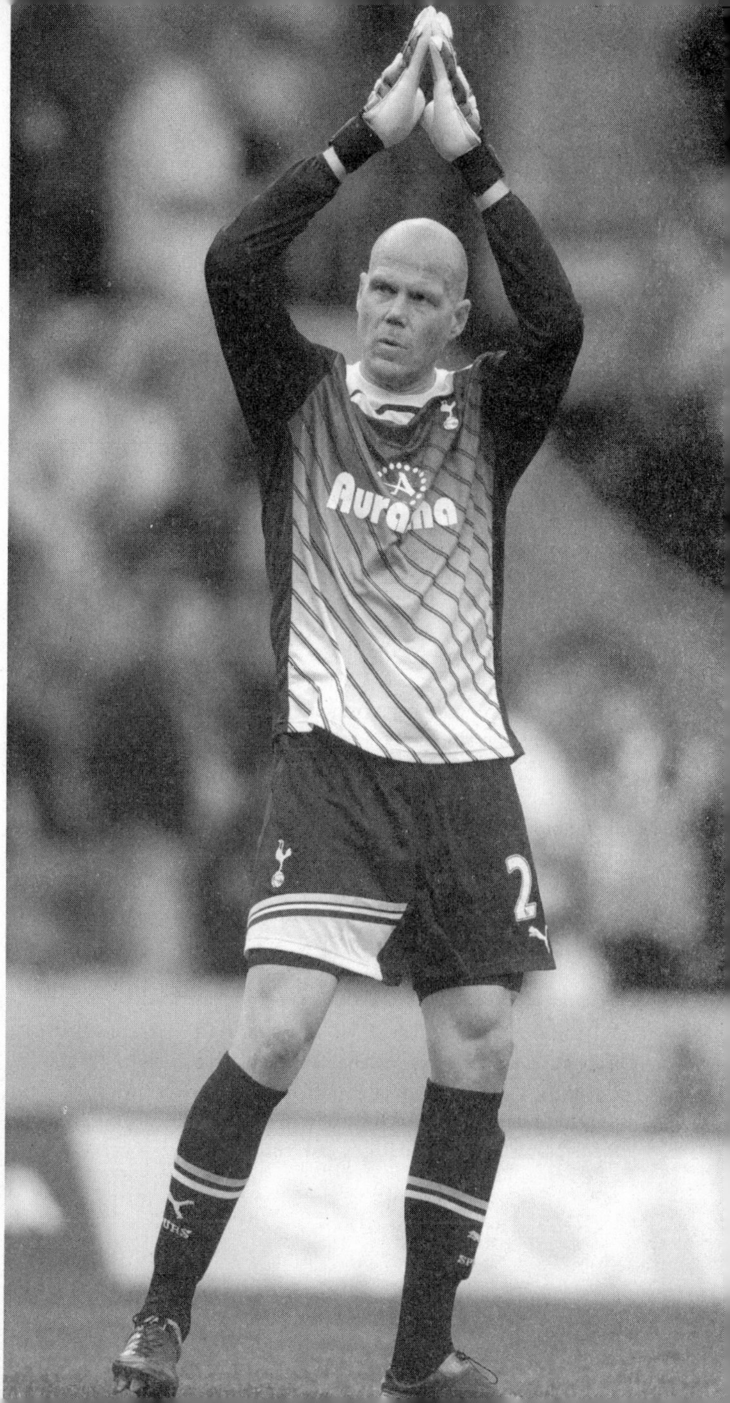

BRAD FRIEDEL JOINED SPURS IN JUNE 2011.

SATURDAY 5th JUNE 1909

Spurs travel to Argentina with Everton to enjoy a post-season tour. The Lilywhites played seven times on the trip to South America, facing the Toffees in the first of those matches. It finished all square with each side scoring twice. Walter Tull and Bert Middlemass were the men to strike for Spurs in rather alien surroundings for the players.

WEDNESDAY 6th JUNE 1979

A mildly farcical occasion was created when Spurs took on a Bermuda XI. The opposition were far inferior to Spurs, which led to a 3-1 victory. Colin Lee, Chris Jones, and Bermudan Alan Marshall got on the score-sheet for Tottenham. The match was more noteworthy for the fact that Spurs' goalkeeper Milija Aleksic played right-wing!

SATURDAY 7th JUNE 1947

Spurs have only once had to play a league match during this month, due to severe mid-season weather issues. Barnsley were the opposition at White Hart Lane and the Tykes closed both clubs' campaign with a hard-earned 1-1 draw. Eddie Jones made his debut for the club, having signed recently from Swansea Town and the Spurs goal came from 12 yards as Ronnie Dix converted a penalty.

SATURDAY 8th JUNE 1957

Celtic provide opposition for four games of Spurs' North American tour. This match against the Bhoys took place in Vancouver, as 24,198 people witness Bobby Smith score his second hat-trick of the trip. It was Smith's goals that made the difference, as Spurs ran out 3-1 winners against the Scots.

WEDNESDAY 9th JUNE 1971

A Japanese XI are defeated 3-0 in Spurs' final game on their tour of Japan. Their previous matches had brought 6-0 and 7-2 victories. This game was slightly tougher, but Martin Chivers' fifth goal of the tour, and two from Alan Mullery, were more than enough to beat the opposition who were, if nothing else, enthusiastic.

WEDNESDAY 10th JUNE 1981

Two matches in Turkey may not have been seen as a great reward for the FA Cup holders, but it gave the Spurs players a different experience of European football. Trabzonspor lost heavily as Spurs scored four goals without reply. Mark Falco, Ricky Villa, Ossie Ardiles and Garth Crooks were all on target in a comfortable victory.

SATURDAY 11th JUNE 1983

Two games against Manchester United were organised to be played in Swaziland as part of the Royal Swazi Sun Challenge. Today's match finishes 2-0 to Spurs as Steve Perryman and Garry Mabbutt score the goals. The first match had been lost 2-1, meaning that the tournament had to be decided on penalties, with Spurs coming out on top.

TUESDAY 12th JUNE 1945

Pat Jennings is born in Newry, Northern Ireland. The goalkeeper arrived at White Hart Lane from Watford in 1964 for a fee of £27,000. He would go on to play for 13 years at Spurs, making 472 league appearances and winning four major honours in the process; Jennings was a member of the League Cup-winning sides of 1971 and 1973, as well as winning the FA Cup in 1967, and Uefa Cup in 1972. He created a little piece of history when he scored a goal in the 1967 FA Charity Shield but at 32 years of age, many thought he was coming to the end of his career – but he shocked everyone at Spurs by moving to arch-rivals Arsenal in 1977. Jennings actually went on to play for another eight seasons and earned a record-breaking 119 caps for Northern Ireland over 22 years.

SUNDAY 12th JUNE 1966

Spurs surprisingly travelled to Mexico expecting to play against some local club sides, but in the end provided the opposition for a warm-up game for their national team as they prepared for the World Cup in England. The 100,000 people that were packed inside the stadium were left slightly disappointed as Alan Gilzean scored the only goal of the game.

WEDNESDAY 13th JUNE 2012

Harry Redknapp is sacked by Spurs despite leading the Lilywhites to two top four finishes in three years. The move shocks the football world and is a major blow for Redknapp who had been snubbed by England earlier in the year – despite the nation clamouring for his appointment.

MONDAY 14th JUNE 1993

One of the fiercest battles in Spurs' history didn't come on the pitch but in the courthouse as Terry Venables and Alan Sugar faced each other in a legal dispute. There was a lot of arguing played out in the media in the time between Venables' sacking and the start of the court case. It was a complex case that bitterly ran for more than a year.

SUNDAY 15th JUNE 1952

Two games in 24 hours against the league champions may have seemed like an arduous task for a football team, but Spurs easily defeated Manchester United 5-0 in the first match, and then topped that with a 7-1 victory the next day. The goals were scored by Len Duquemin (4), Les Bennett (2) and Sid McClellan.

THURSDAY 16th JUNE 1983

It was a historical day for Spurs when it was announced that the club would be floated on the Stock Exchange as they aimed to raise enough money to wipe off debts. The gamble paid off as the stock was three-and-a-half times oversubscribed with many loyal fans being allowed to purchase shares, and have their say on club matters.

WEDNESDAY 17th JUNE 1908

Spurs fail to win election into the Football League. It wasn't as simple a process as it should have been, considering the club had won the FA Cup some seven years earlier. In an original vote, they lost out to Bradford for the one available place, but circumstances favoured Spurs as Stoke had to resign their position due to financial problems, creating an opening for the north Londoners in the Second Division. At last, the Lilywhites had finally arrived.

FANS' FAVOURITE OSSIE ARDILES RETURNED TO SPURS AS BOSS IN JUNE 1993.

WEDNESDAY 18th JUNE 1952

Facing Quebec wasn't the most difficult prospect for FA Cup holders Spurs, as their tour of North America came to a conclusion. Ninety minutes and eight goals later, Spurs had strolled to a simple victory. Hat-tricks from Sid McClellan and Les Bennett, plus solo strikes from Ralph Wetton and Les Medley, did the damage.

SATURDAY 19th JUNE 1993

Ossie Ardiles' return to Spurs provided the fanfare needed to push Terry Venables' controversial sacking into the background. The Argentine was still a hero at White Hart Lane thanks to his extraordinary playing career with the club. Alan Sugar got his man, who was managing West Bromwich Albion at the time, hoping it would return him to his previous level of popularity that he enjoyed with fans. Sadly, it didn't work out as Spurs finished his first season in 15th. Three months into his second season he was sacked. Ardiles then set off on a nomadic managerial career all around the world, taking charge of another ten clubs over a 14-year period but tellingly, never lasting more than two years at any of them.

SUNDAY 20th JUNE 1909

Spurs win the final game of their South American tour by defeating Argentinian side Rosario 9-0. Unfortunately, no-one kept the records of any more specific information for the game, as only the scoreline was recorded by those on the trip, especially considering the fact all the other results on the tour were noted with some detail. Maybe a Rosario official took the notes as a favour…

SATURDAY 21st JUNE 1947

Having already suffered two defeats on their end-of-season sojourn around France, it was important to regain some pride and so it proved as Spurs defeated St Etienne 2-0 in the French city. The crucial goals were scored by Les Bennett and Charlie Rundle; the two had very different careers with the club. Bennett played almost 300 times, while Rundle only appeared on 28 occasions.

WEDNESDAY 21st JUNE 1989

Gary Lineker signs from Barcelona for £1.2m. The striker would go on to make 105 appearances in three years, scoring 60 goals in the process. In his first season with the club he scored 24 times, making him the First Division's top scorer, as Spurs finished in third position. He was part of the 1991 FA Cup-winning team and will be remembered for missing a penalty in the final. Lineker left the club in 1992 to sign for Japanese outfit Nagoya Grampus Eight and seemed to spend the majority of his time there nursing a broken toe!

SATURDAY 22nd JUNE 1991

The club was saved from extinction as local boy Alan Sugar completes his £7.25m takeover of Spurs. Crippling debts were the problem, as years of mismanagement had caused the club to make severe losses year after year, which couldn't be offset by the club's relative on-field success, having just won the FA Cup. Alan, Sir Alan and now Lord Alan would enjoy mixed fortunes during his tenure, but had enough troubled times to claim he'd never enter into the world of football again, instead becoming a hugely popular TV celebrity in BBC 1's *The Apprentice*.

WEDNESDAY 23rd JUNE 1909

The Spurs players loved their football, and with their day off on a tour of South America, they decided to take in a local game to witness the different footballing cultures. When a pitch invasion was instigated, the Spurs players were taken aback when the police's cavalry division took to the field with swords drawn to remove the trespassers! Needless to say, they opted against joining the pitch trespassing.

THURSDAY 24th JUNE 1965

Spurs play Israeli sided Maccabi Tel-Aviv in the John White Cup, being played in the honour of the club legend known as 'The Ghost' who had tragically died after being struck by lightning the previous summer at the age of 27. Fittingly Tottenham were victorious, thanks to goals from three of their most consistent performers; Alan Mullery, Dave Mackay and Alan Gilzean scored in the 3-2 win.

MONDAY 25th JUNE 1973

Jamie Redknapp, son of former West Ham United midfielder and future Tottenham manager Harry, is born in Barton-on-Sea, England. Redknapp junior made a name for himself at AFC Bournemouth, who were being managed by his father at the time, before Liverpool boss Kenny Dalglish snapped up the young prodigy at the age of 17 in a £350,000 deal, making Redknapp one of the most expensive teenagers in Britain at the time. While at Anfield, he made 308 appearances scoring 41 goals and won 17 caps for England before moving to Spurs on a free transfer. Injuries took their toll on Redknapp's career and he was forced to retire early.

MONDAY 25th JUNE 1984

Peter Shreeves is promoted from the role of assistant manager, to take over from Keith Burkinshaw as manager of Spurs. He had been associated with the club for a decade having started out as youth-team coach and then reserves' boss. He became Burkinshaw's second in command for four seasons before being handed the reins. In Shreeves' two seasons in charge, the team finished third and tenth respectively, but he was still removed from his position.

FRIDAY 26th JUNE 1998

When England took on Colombia at the 1998 World Cup in France, Spurs could boast a strong connection to the national team, with Darren Anderton scoring the first under the management of former club legend Glenn Hoddle. Anderton's inclusion was something of a surprise to many considering he had only managed 15 club appearances all season due to – you guessed it – injury.

FRIDAY 27th JUNE 2008

Heurelho Gomes signs from PSV Eindhoven. The Brazilian was signed as a replacement for Paul Robinson who had become error prone in recent times. Gomes had built a reputation in Holland for being a great shot stopper and Juande Ramos jumped at the chance to sign him. Unfortunately, he didn't adapt well to the Premier League and cost his side points on numerous occasions in the early part of his Spurs career. He soon improved, but on the run-in to the 2010/11 campaign, he had several high-profile gaffs, causing a fed-up Harry Redknapp to sign Brad Friedel on a free transfer.

THURSDAY 28th JUNE 2012

Tottenham superstar Gareth Bale pledges his future to the club by signing a new four-year contract and in turn warding off interest of Real Madrid, Barcelona and Manchester United.

MONDAY 29th JUNE 1908

Spurs' place in the Football League is finally confirmed after a recent defeat to Bradford in the election for the one official place, but thanks to Stoke's resignation from the Second Division, the club were finally granted the opportunity to continue their progress as a professional outfit in a national competition. There had been an anxious wait to have the promotion rubber-stamped as the Football League reluctantly welcomed the Lilywhites to its family.

FRIDAY 29th JUNE 2007

Spurs break their transfer record to bring Darren Bent to the club from Charlton Athletic. The striker costs £16.5m when he makes the move from The Valley. Bent never managed to hold down one of the club's striking roles, as he was unable to convince Harry Redknapp that he was the man to spearhead the club's attack. Even though he was never a first-team regular, he scored 18 goals in 60 league appearances for Spurs. He left after two seasons at the club, before Sunderland took him away from London for the same fee that Spurs had paid for his services. He continues his nomadic career in yet another huge deal to Aston Villa.

FRIDAY 30th JUNE 1995

Spurs act quickly to replace the outgoing Jurgen Klinsmann by splashing out £4.5m on the prolific Crystal Palace striker, Chris Armstrong. Despite early criticism of the signing, Armstrong did reasonably well with Spurs and formed a successful partnership with Teddy Sheringham. Unfortunately, he would never have the ability or charisma of his German predecessor, and would eventually leave the club in 2002 after a collection of injuries ruined his later years with the club.

SPURS
On This Day

JULY

MONDAY 1st JULY 1935

Jack Tresadern is appointed Spurs manager. He had previously been in charge at Northampton Town, Burnley and Crystal Palace before taking on the job at White Hart Lane. His spell in north London was not successful, winning few games and being an unpopular figure with all connected to Spurs for one reason or another. He toughed it out for almost three years before he eventually left in 1938 to take the same position at Plymouth Argyle.

SATURDAY 1st JULY 1995

Spurs never had much interest in the Intertoto Cup, but were forced to enter by the Football Association after meeting the qualification criteria. A strange mixture of fringe players, youngsters and loan players made up the Spurs squad and all home games were played at Brighton & Hove Albion. Their first victory came in their second outing against Slovenian side, Rudar Velenje.

THURSDAY 1st JULY 2004

Jacques Santini arrives to take over as Spurs manager. The Frenchman had agreed to take the reins at White Hart Lane the previous month, but was the French national team manager at the time, so had to see out the summer's European Championships. Things did not work out for him, as he only managed 13 games in charge of the club before resigning, citing family problems as a reason to quit north London.

SATURDAY 2nd JULY 1994

Chairman Alan Sugar took his appeal against a £600,000 fine, 12-point deduction and FA Cup ban to the Football Association. Sugar felt the punishment was too harsh for the crimes committed. The points penalty was halved, but the fine was more than doubled to £1,500,000.

TUESDAY 3rd JULY 2012

Andre Villas-Boas becomes the new Spurs boss after agreeing a three-year contract. The former Porto and Chelsea manager is initially viewed with suspicion by the Tottenham faithful but a solid first six months with some impressive tactical victories soon allays fears.

SATURDAY 4th JULY 1946

Eugene 'Taffy' O'Callaghan passes away. A star of the late 1920s and early 1930s, Taffy signed professional forms in September 1926 and made his debut in the following January at Everton. He went on to play 252 games for the Lilywhites, scoring 92 goals, before leaving for Leicester City in 1935.

MONDAY 5th JULY 1982

There was heightened tension between England and Argentina due to the ongoing conflict in the Falklands. This forced the club's hand as they decided to loan out Ossie Ardiles to French club Paris St Germain to ensure he avoided any reprisals from emotional fans. In the end, Ardiles only stayed in France for six months, before returning to London to take his place in the Spurs team.

TUESDAY 6th JULY 1993

Two former club greats return to Spurs in coaching capacities, ironically at the expense of another legendary figure. Steve Perryman came in as Ossie Ardiles' assistant manager, whilst Pat Jennings was appointed as goalkeeping coach, replacing Ray Clemence. Former assistant manager Doug Livermore became the club's head of scouting in the backroom staff shake-up.

THURSDAY 7th JULY 1994

With the club suffering a mini-crisis due to the punishments inflicted upon them, they were struggling to attract players, a situation which was summed up when former apprentice Vinny Samways requested a transfer. The midfielder was sold to Everton and ironically made his debut at White Hart Lane on the opening day of the season.

SATURDAY 7th JULY 2011

Press reports suggest Spurs are chasing 'the new Luka Modric'. The Hajduk Split forward Ante Vukusic is valued at £8m but the Lilywhites face competition from other Premier League clubs. Rather than replace Modric, the subject of several bids from Chelsea, Redknapp is reported to want Vukusic to play in tandem with the Croat. The 20-year-old scored 20 goals for Split but, interestingly, holds Modric as his idol.

TUESDAY 8th JULY 1980

Robbie Keane is born in Dublin, Ireland. Rafael Benitez brought the Irishman to Liverpool in a £19m deal from Spurs on July 28th 2008 after Keane had built a reputation as being one of the most prolific strikers in the Premier League – he was also a boyhood Red. He began his career at Wolverhampton Wanderers before moving to Coventry City in 1999. After a year at Highfield Road, he moved to Inter Milan, managed at the time by World Cup winner Marco Tardelli. Keane spent just one season in Italy before moving back to England where he joined Leeds United. Spurs paid £7m for his services in 2002 and he became an integral member of the squad at White Hart Lane for six seasons. He netted 107 goals in 254 games for Spurs before joining Liverpool where he could only manage seven goals in 28 appearances. He rejoined Tottenham in January 2009 for £12m, later playing for West Ham United and then LA Galaxy in 2011.

SUNDAY 8th JULY 1990

Jurgen Klinsmann becomes a World Cup winner as his West Germany side defeat Argentina in Italy with Andreas Brehme scoring the winner from the penalty spot.

MONDAY 9th JULY 1883

Legendary goalkeeper Tommy Lunn was born in Bishop Auckland. He started his career at Wolverhampton Wanderers where he made his name before signing for a Spurs side facing relegation from the top flight in April 1910. Lunn played in the final two games of the campaign, which garnered maximum points for Spurs with the goalkeeper being credited as one of the main reasons for these victories.

MONDAY 10th JULY 1978

It was possibly the transfer coup of the decade as two World Cup winners agreed to join Spurs; Ossie Ardiles and Ricky Villa had won the competition only weeks previously with Argentina and the excitement the transfers caused was approaching fever pitch by the season's kick-off. After adapting to the style of English football, the two men become firm favourites with the White Hart Lane faithful, as they played pivotal roles at the club in their time in London.

MONDAY 11th JULY 1966

Going into the World Cup, Jimmy Greaves was the focal point of the England attack. He started all three of the team's group games, before succumbing to injury in the final game against France. Greaves hadn't scored in his three outings which was a factor in him being omitted from the team that won the final 4-2, as Geoff Hurst was selected instead. The rest, as they say, is history.

THURSDAY 12th JULY 1956

Tony Galvin is born in Yorkshire and goes on to become one of Spurs' finest wingers. The club paid just £30,000 for his services from non-league Goole Town in 1978. He wasn't your typical footballer, either, having recently completed a degree in Russian studies and a teaching training course. After a slow start with the club, he established himself in the early stages of 1981 and was in the side that won the FA Cup that year. He left for Sheffield Wednesday in 1987.

THURSDAY 13th JULY 2001

Steffen Freund scores his one and only goal as a Spurs player. His strike in a pre-season friendly against Stevenage wasn't witnessed by many, but he enjoyed his celebrations in the 8-1 win. Throughout his entire career, the German midfielder only managed nine goals, and none of those were in his 102 league games for Spurs. Shooooot!

WEDNESDAY 14th JULY 1976

Keith Burkinshaw is appointed as the club's manager after Terry Neill decided to resign, following disagreements with the Spurs hierarchy whilst on a pre-season tour in Australia. Neill quickly moved on to take the manager's job at Arsenal, much to the Spurs fans' disdain. After a slow start to his career in charge at White Hart Lane, things soon picked up, and he led them to four trophy successes. He eventually left in 1984 when he fell out with the club's new board, but left with his head held high. His standing at the club is unquestioned with his 1981 FA Cup success over Manchester City an undoubted highlight.

TUESDAY 15th JULY 1998

New signing Paolo Tramezzani makes his debut in a 6-0 win at Peterborough United, scoring the opening goal at London Road. He lasts less than a year at White Hart Lane after failing to make an impression on either the manager who signed him, Christian Gross, or his replacement, George Graham.

SUNDAY 16th JULY 1995

Spurs' mixture of loan players and youngsters faced Osters IF of Sweden in an Intertoto Cup group game. The Swedes defeated the inexperienced Spurs side 2-1. It was a chance for the youngsters, with only Stephen Carr from the side going on to have a prosperous career with the club. The Tottenham goalscorer on the day was Gerard McMahon who played a few times for the first team, but never really established himself.

SATURDAY 17th JULY 1999

A pre-season tour of Sweden was the perfect place for the returning Tottenham players to find form against a selection of mediocre opponents. One man who benefited from the trip was young Steffen Iversen, who bagged 11 goals prior to the start of the season. This included a hat-trick against Lysekils FF in a 7-1 victory for Tottenham. It seemed to be a springboard for Iversen, as he went on to have his best season for the club, scoring 14 league goals.

TUESDAY 17th JULY 2001

Attacking left-back Christian Ziege joins Spurs after just one season with Liverpool. Capped 72 times, the German international's time at White Hart Lane is dogged by injury, though he has one or two highlights, such as scoring in the 2002 League Cup Final, and was more than useful to have around dead-ball situations. In three years he made only 47 league appearances, scoring seven goals, before having his contract mutually terminated in 2004. He returned to play a handful of games for Borussia Monchengladbach, eventually moving into coaching after his retirement following a persistent ankle problem.

FRIDAY 18th JULY 1997

New signing David Ginola arrives at Tottenham overweight and in need of games to improve his fitness levels. His first appearance was in Sweden when Spurs took on Fredrikstad in pre-season when he came on to replace Ruel Fox for the final 25 minutes.

THURSDAY 19th JULY 2001

Glenn Hoddle was trying to stamp his mark on Tottenham during pre-season. They played a collection of games against lower league English teams. Versus Leyton Orient they ran out 2-0 winners with Sergei Rebrov and Simon Davies doing the damage. Rebrov, the new Ukrainian signing, flattered to deceive as he followed up an impressive pre-season with a poor league campaign in which he failed to establish himself in the team.

SUNDAY 20th JULY 2003

Bobby Zamora makes his first appearance for the club against Oxford United at the Kassam Stadium, having signed two days previously for around £1.5m from Brighton & Hove Albion. His impact was almost instant as he netted twice in the first half. Sadly, he never lived up to his promise in the Premier League, and was seen as no more than a fringe player, before leaving for West Ham United where he blossomed into a leading marksman and future England player. Zamora is seen by many as a confidence player – when he's on his game, he's virtually unplayable, when he's off form he can be something of a passenger. As of 2008, he plied his trade with Fulham where he seems to have found his spiritual home.

TUESDAY 21st JULY 1964

Johnny White was one of the club's finest players at the time, and his death is one of the most tragic moments in Spurs' history. As well as being a great footballer, he was also a good golfer and would spend many hours playing at Crews Hill Golf Club in Enfield. White died at the club aged 27, when the tree he was sheltering from the rain under was struck by lightning whilst in the middle of a round of golf. He left behind a wife and two children.

JOHN WHITE – SEEN HERE IN ACTION IN THE 1961 FA CUP FINAL – WAS TRAGICALLY KILLED, WHEN HE WAS STRUCK BY LIGHTNING IN JULY 1964.

THURSDAY 22nd JULY 1993

Neil 'Razor' Ruddock joins Liverpool in a deal worth £2.5m from Tottenham, where he'd been in his second spell, and enjoyed an excellent 12 months. The tough, uncompromising defender cut an imposing figure on the pitch and his no-nonsense approach made him a player you either loved or hated. He had ability and could ping accurate passes to turn defence into attack with great effect and it's fair to say he enjoyed every minute of his time at White Hart Lane, and later Anfield. Ruddock played 152 times and scored 12 goals before returning to London – initially on loan with QPR – before signing permanently for West Ham United in 1998.

SATURDAY 22nd JULY 1995

The comedy of the Intertoto Cup campaign finally came to an end, as the reserve side was sent to Germany where they suffered an embarrassing 8-0 defeat at the hands of Cologne. The club always stated that they would not field their strongest XI in any game and that it was – as far as they were concerned – a reserve-team competition. The result was still embarrassing for a club of Spurs' stature.

WEDNESDAY 23rd JULY 1991

Peter Shreeves becomes the club's manager for the second time, as he replaces Terry Venables who is now Spurs' chief executive. He had previously taken charge of the first team for two seasons in the mid-1980s, and like that period, this would be deeply unsuccessful, as he was removed from his job after only a year in charge.

FRIDAY 24th JULY 1992

Spurs travelled to Scotland in order to take on Hearts, and it was a Scot who caused most damage in the shape of Gordon Durie, who scored twice in a 2-1 win. He was the club's only senior striker, as Gary Lineker had left White Hart Lane in the summer in order to move to Nagoya Grampus Eight of Japan. As for Durie, he stayed with Spurs for a couple of seasons but averaged just one goal every six games before moving to Rangers in 1993.

SATURDAY 25th JULY 1987

A Spurs XI travelled to Dean Court to play AFC Bournemouth in a pre-season friendly. It was a successful practice match for the attack, as they bagged four, but the defence had a trickier time, conceding the same amount in an entertaining 4-4 draw. Chris Waddle, Steve Hodge and Clive Allen (2) were the men on the score-sheet for Tottenham against the Cherries.

SATURDAY 26th JULY 2003

Spurs leave for South Africa with the intention of playing two matches – and return with a new midfielder. In a game against the national champions, Orlando Pirates, the Spurs management team were so impressed with their captain, Mbulelo Mabizela, that they decided to sign him. His time in London wasn't successful, as he only managed seven appearances for Spurs, before being released from his contract after only 14 months in England.

WEDNESDAY 27th JULY 1994

Ilie Dumitrescu arrived at the club after being one of the stars of the recent World Cup in the USA. Manager Ossie Ardiles saw his purchase as a vital cog in his Spurs midfield, but unfortunately he couldn't find him a suitable role in the team's formation. He only managed two seasons with the club, making 17 appearances, which included time out on loan with Seville in Spain. In 1996 he was sold to neighbours West Ham United.

SUNDAY 28th JULY 2002

Famous double-winning left-back Ron Henry's grandson Ronnie didn't make the kind of mark for the club he and his family would have loved, with his main senior contribution being the opening goal in a pre-season friendly against Queens Park Rangers at Loftus Road. He never played first-team football for Spurs, but has managed to make a successful career for himself in the Football League with Stevenage. As for Ronnie's grandfather, he joined Spurs in 1952, and made his debut in 1955 as a centre-half, switching to left-back after a short time. Overall, Henry played 247 league games for the Lilywhites, scoring one goal.

TUESDAY 28th JULY 2009

Former Spurs youngster Peter Crouch returns to the club almost a decade after leaving for Queens Park Rangers. Since then the 6ft 7in striker has gone on to play for Aston Villa, Liverpool and Portsmouth in the Premier League whilst also being an England regular under a variety of international managers. His stay at White Hart Lane was relatively short, joining Stoke City on transfer deadline day in August 2011.

FRIDAY 29th JULY 1994

Jurgen Klinsmann left the tax haven of Monaco to sign for Tottenham after the 1994 World Cup. He would be a pivotal part of Spurs' attacking force in the season to come, as he scored 21 goals. The German left at the end of the campaign to return to his native Germany to play for Bayern Munich. Klinsmann was appointed as the manager of the USA in August 2011.

WEDNESDAY 30th JULY 2008

David Bentley signs for a club-record fee of £15m from Blackburn Rovers, with the potential for the transfer cost to rise to £17m. The former Arsenal youngster was brought in to add width and supply the club's strikers with pinpoint crosses. He never managed to cement a place in the team, mainly due to the fine form of Aaron Lennon, only making 43 appearances in his first three seasons with the club, which included a loan spell at Birmingham City. Bentley also has seven international caps for England and joined West Ham United in 2011.

WEDNESDAY 31st JULY 2011

Jermain Defoe declares that he would rather go out on loan than sit on the Spurs bench. The England striker, concerned about his Euro 2012 place in the England squad, adds that if he begins as a sub for the first few weeks of the 2011/12 campaign, he will look for pastures new, albeit on a temporary basis.

SPURS
On This Day

AUGUST

SATURDAY 1st AUGUST 1992

As part of the deal that brought Gerard McMahon to Spurs, the club agrees to travel to Northern Ireland to face his former side Glenavon in a friendly. Guest of honour Terry Venables opens the part-timers' new main stand at Mourneview Park. The actual match sees Spurs beat the County Armagh outfit thanks to the only goal of the game from midfielder Vinny Samways.

SATURDAY 2nd AUGUST 1997

David Howells had been a great servant for Spurs over the years and is rewarded a testimonial. He played 335 times in over a decade at the club. Howells began his Spurs career as a striker, but gradually moved back and established himself playing in a defensive midfield role. But, he never lost his ability to score, netting 27 goals in total. A decent turnout of 14,605 attend and see new recruits David Ginola and Les Ferdinand for the first time in the game against Fiorentina, but the Italians spoil Howell's farewell match, running out 2-0 winners courtesy of goals from Andrei Kanchelskis and Luis Oliveira.

SUNDAY 3rd AUGUST 1952

Ossie Ardiles is born in Bell Ville, Argentina. The midfielder played the early part of his career at Instituto de Córdoba and Belgrano before his talents were spotted by Huracán, where he would spend the next three years of his career. Ardiles spent a decade with Spurs after signing in 1978, making 221 league appearances. As a player, he won the World Cup, two FA Cups and a Uefa Cup. He would return to Spurs in 1993 as manager, but could not repeat the success of his playing days and only managed a year in charge at White Hart Lane. He remains a club legend.

SATURDAY 3rd AUGUST 1974

Spurs travel to Edinburgh to face Scottish Premier League Hearts in their first pre-season match of the summer, at Tynecastle. Both teams fail to get into their stride with the rust showing and fitness levels somewhat wanting. The game finished a 1-1 draw with Spurs' strike coming from substitute John Pratt – who Hearts claimed to be offside – in vain.

SATURDAY 4th AUGUST 1984

Enfield is only a short distance away from Tottenham geographically, but in footballing terms it's a world away, as was proved in a pre-season friendly. Spurs notch seven without reply, with the goals coming from Gary Stevens, Micky Hazard, Garry Brooke and Garth Crooks, who got four for himself. Interestingly, Ossie Ardiles' friend, and fellow World Cup winner, Mario Kempes was on trial with the Lilywhites, but failed to impress and was not offered a contract.

SATURDAY 5th AUGUST 1967

A glamorous friendly against the European Cup winners Celtic takes place at Hampden Park. Spurs had just lifted the FA Cup, so both teams were seen as powerhouses on the continent and the match was billed in the press as 'The Battle of Britain'. The match attracts tremendous interest and more than 90,000 people fill the ground – and they didn't leave disappointed as the matched finished 3-3. Jimmy Greaves nets twice, scoring either side of an Alan Gilzean goal, in a thrilling spectacle.

SATURDAY 6th AUGUST 1994

Jurgen Klinsmann makes his debut for Spurs in a friendly at Vicarage Road as Spurs played against Watford. The German didn't score in the match, but showed glimpses of the class that Spurs could expect to see in the season to come. The game ended in a 1-1 draw, but the thousands of Spurs fans who had come to see him play for the Lilywhites leave satisfied in the knowledge the club had spent wisely.

SATURDAY 7th AUGUST 1999

Spurs have a nightmare start to the season at Upton Park after George Graham takes a side riddled with injuries to face West Ham United. Sol Campbell had to be replaced after 30 minutes due to a muscle problem and the Hammers were in the lead before half-time. The team couldn't find a way back, and Justin Edinburgh was forced to leave the pitch with 20 minutes to go, leaving Spurs with only ten men on the pitch, as all their subs had been used.

SATURDAY 8th AUGUST 1981

A full strength Tottenham XI take on Northern Irish outfit Glentoran in a warm-up match for the upcoming season. The opposition were far from pushovers and shared the spoils in a six-goal thriller. Glenn Hoddle, Mark Falco and Ossie Ardiles got their names on the score-sheet to guarantee that Spurs weren't embarrassed against the part-timers who more than held their own on the day.

SATURDAY 9th AUGUST 1969

Spurs have a disappointing start to the new season as they are easily beaten by Leeds United at Elland Road. The only bright point for Tottenham was the return to fitness of Martin Chivers, who had missed the majority of the previous campaign with injury. Even Big Chiv couldn't find the back of the net on his comeback, with Jimmy Greaves scoring Spurs' consolation in a 3-1 loss.

SATURDAY 10th AUGUST 1991

It was a re-run of the previous season's FA Cup semi-final as Spurs faced local rivals Arsenal in the season's opener, the Charity Shield at Wembley. The curtain raiser between the FA Cup winners and the First Division champions ends ended goalless, with the two sides sharing the shield – and the bragging rights.

SUNDAY 10th AUGUST 1997

Les Ferdinand makes his Spurs debut against Manchester United. His £6m fee was seen to be quite high for a 30-year-old striker, but Ferdinand was ecstatic to have signed for his boyhood club. Things didn't quite go to plan, as he missed a good proportion of the season through injury, but his return to the team sparked a revival, as Spurs avoided relegation with 'Sir Les', as he was christened by QPR fans, spearheading the recovery alongside Jurgen Klinsmann. He also scored the Premier League's 10,000th goal in 2001 in a game against Fulham but his six-year stay at White Hart Lane was spoiled by a catalogue of injuries. Ferdinand would eventually leave the club in 2003 to join West Ham United wondering just how high he may have flown had he managed to steer clear of the fitness problems that dogged his latter years.

SATURDAY 11th AUGUST 1962

Spurs come up against newly-crowned league champions Ipswich Town in the Charity Shield knowing that they had lost twice to the side from Portman Road in the league the previous season. However, that had no effect on the Spurs team, as they romped home 5-1 to send a warning to the rest of Division One that the deposed title holders were far from a spent force. Jimmy Greaves hits two goals, with Terry Medwin, Johnny White and Bobby Smith netting the others to give the Shield to Tottenham.

THURSDAY 11th AUGUST 2011

With the start of the season only days away, Spurs had their opener against Everton postponed due to rioting and public disorder in the north London area. Mass looting and running battles with the police began earlier in the week, with buildings suffering serious damage in the trouble. It was decided that for security reasons it would be best to cancel the match as police were concerned that they couldn't guarantee the safety of fans. Few disagreed with the decision, particularly with no obvious indications that the disturbances were over.

SATURDAY 12th AUGUST 1961

Having won a historic double the previous season, Spurs had no opposition for the Charity Shield as they had dominated domestic football, winning both major honours – rather than play themselves and a change from the usual routine, the Football Association put a stellar XI together to take on the all-conquering Lilywhites. The side were still no match for Tottenham as they won 3-2 thanks to two strikes from Les Allen and a goal from Bobby Smith.

SATURDAY 12th AUGUST 1967

Pat Jennings performed heroics in the Spurs goal for years to keep out the opposition, but he finally found out what it was like to score himself when Spurs took on Manchester United in the Charity Shield. His long clearance bounced in between Alan Gilzean and goalkeeper Alex Stepney with the ball looping over his head and into the back of the net. The other strikes came from Jimmy Robertson and Frank Saul, but United scored the same amount to force a draw, and the sharing of the Shield in a thrilling 3-3 draw.

WEDNESDAY 13th AUGUST 1969

Spurs dismantle a talented Burnley side at White Hart Lane by scoring four goals without reply. Peter Collins, Jimmy Pearce, Jimmy Greaves and Martin Chivers were the men who made the difference on the day, all netting once each to make sure they gained the advantage heading into the second leg of this League Cup tie.

SATURDAY 14th AUGUST 1993

Ossie Ardiles' first game in charge – at Newcastle United. Ironically, the Argentine had previously had a spell as the Magpies' manager, but was sacked after one season in charge. Ardiles got his revenge as Tottenham gained the three points thanks to a 1-0 win at St James' Park, with Teddy Sheringham netting the decisive goal.

SATURDAY 14th AUGUST 2011

A Joe Hart wonder show earns Manchester City a point at Tottenham and sets the Blues up for a solid season that will ultimately see them pip Harry Redknapp's side to a Champions League spot. Four of Hart's saves in the first half are world class while Spurs fans are left scratching their heads as to how their team haven't won by three or four goals.

MONDAY 15th AUGUST 1960

Danny Blanchflower was well respected on and off the pitch and his appearance on the national institution radio show that is *Desert Island Discs* proves to be hugely popular. The midfielder had an enjoyable half hour on the show, with presenter Roy Plomley. His luxury item is a golf club, and some balls, to pass his time on the island!

SUNDAY 15th AUGUST 1965

Spurs took part in a pre-season tournament, the Costa del Sol Trophy, held in Malaga. On this occasion, Tottenham start the competition well by defeating Valencia in the first match 2-1, with Eddie Clayton and Cliff Jones scoring the goals. The Lilywhites then went on to beat Standard Liege in the final, with Alan Mullery making the difference in a 1-0 victory to win their first silverware of the fledgling campaign.

SATURDAY 16th AUGUST 1980

Keith Burkinshaw's side host Nottingham Forest on the opening day of the season, giving the White Hart Lane faithful an opportunity to see the club's new arrivals. The dream strike partnership of Steve Archibald and Garth Crooks both make their debuts in the 2-0 win and Crooks also manages to get a goal in his first appearance in a Spurs shirt, adding to Glenn Hoddle's earlier strike.

SATURDAY 17th AUGUST 1996

Ewood Park is the venue for Spurs' first game of the campaign, but a 2-0 win came at a cost when captain Garry Mabbutt breaks his leg after 20 minutes. It didn't deter his team-mates, as Chris Armstrong scored soon after his skipper was stretchered off and later added another, but despite the victory, the shattering news that Mabbutt would not play again that season soon put paid to the gloss of the victory over Blackburn Rovers.

MONDAY 18th AUGUST 1952

Ricardo 'Ricky' Villa is born in Roque Pérez, Argentina. He made over 200 appearances in his homeland, before moving to England in 1978, having just won the World Cup. Villa played in 133 league games for Spurs, becoming a club legend thanks to his wonder goal in the 1981 FA Cup Final against Manchester City. In 2008, he was inducted into the club's Hall of Fame to commemorate his success with the club.

SATURDAY 18th AUGUST 1971

Newcastle's visit to White Hart Lane ends in a 0-0 draw, but there were still plenty of headlines about the game in the next day's papers with the match severely overshadowed by crowd violence. The referee stops the game for several minutes after the Newcastle goalkeeper is struck by an object from the Park Lane End, with the stand being subsequently closed for the following matches.

SATURDAY 18th AUGUST 2007

Spurs make a rip-roaring start against Derby County to go 3-0 up inside 14 minutes at White Hart Lane. Steed Malbranque scores twice in the first six minutes while Jermaine Jenas and Darren Bent add the others.

THURSDAY 18th AUGUST 2011

Spurs defeat Hearts 5-0 at Tynecastle to take a commanding lead from the first leg of their Europa League tie. The English visitors were dominant from kick-off and went three goals ahead thanks to strikes from Rafael van der Vaart, Jermain Defoe and Jake Livermore. In the second period, Spurs continue to control the match against the sluggish Jambos with Gareth Bale and Aaron Lennon adding their names to the score-sheet to complete the rout and all-but guarantee a place in the Europa League group stages.

SATURDAY 19th AUGUST 1978

Spurs' first game on the return to the top flight is against Brian Clough's Nottingham Forest at the City Ground. New signings Ricky Villa and Ossie Ardiles make their debuts under the watchful eye of the world's media, as a new-look Spurs side look to show they were up for a tough season in the league. Villa made an immediate impact, scoring the equaliser late on to grab a well-deserved point for his new club.

SATURDAY 20th AUGUST 1994

Jurgen Klinsmann's infamous 'diving' celebration is seen for the first time in England as he notches a goal on his debut against Sheffield Wednesday at Hillsborough. In what was a pulsating game, Spurs came out on top in a 4-3 win. Ossie Ardiles' attacking mentality was there for all to see as he plays with no less than five forwards, having Ilie Dumitrescu, Nick Barmby, Darren Anderton and Teddy Sheringham alongside the German. The latter three also netted a goal each in the victory over the Owls.

SATURDAY 21st AUGUST 1982

As FA Cup winners, Spurs were given the task of facing league champions Liverpool in the Charity Shield at Wembley. The opposition weren't in particularly charitable mood with some stern challenges flying in early doors – one causing an injury to Tony Galvin. Spurs eventually go down 1-0, with the result less important than the cost of what was, at times, a surprisingly savage game containing little or no charity!

SATURDAY 22nd AUGUST 1981

A new era begins for Spurs as England and former Liverpool legend Ray Clemence makes his debut in goal in the season's curtain raiser at Wembley. The goalkeeper had recently arrived from Anfield for £300,000 and replaced the previous incumbent, Milija Aleksic, between the sticks. A Mark Falco brace was matched by a Peter Withe double in an exciting 2-2 draw played out in front of 92,500 fans meaning yet another drawn Charity Shield match for the Lilywhites.

WEDNESDAY 23rd AUGUST 1978

The excitement about the home debuts of World Cup winners Ricky Villa and Ossie Ardiles was approaching fever pitch in north London, but Aston Villa were unwilling to play to the script as they defeat Spurs 4-1 at White Hart Lane. The only consolation for the Spurs faithful was a Glenn Hoddle penalty, but the supporters' spirits dip, wondering if the stellar Argentine duo might have a disruptive effect on the team rather than a positive influence.

TUESDAY 24th AUGUST 1994

Spurs fans get their first glimpse of Jurgen Klinsmann at White Hart Lane as Everton come to town. Unsurprisingly, the match was a sell-out and the German superstar didn't disappoint, scoring an exquisite volley in the first half to give his new team the lead. Unwilling to settle for just one, the striker added a second to the delight of the home support, as Spurs won 2-1 to complete a dream home start for the German striker.

SATURDAY 25th AUGUST 1990

Two of England's World Cup heroes from the summer are once again reunited in the white shirts of Tottenham, as Paul Gascoigne and Gary Lineker line up at White Hart Lane for a home clash with Manchester City. The two men turn in terrific displays with Gazza getting the first, before Lineker got two more to give Spurs the three points in a 3-1 victory.

RAY CLEMENCE JOINED SPURS IN THE SUMMER OF 1981 AND MADE HIS DEBUT IN AUGUST IN THE CHARITY SHIELD.

SATURDAY 25th AUGUST 1993

Liverpool see their 100% start to the 1993/94 season end as Tottenham record only their third win in 48 visits to Anfield. In the coupon-busting match, Nigel Clough opens the scoring for the hosts who had won their opening three matches, but Teddy Sheringham levels from the penalty spot on 30 minutes and later drives home the winner on 78 minutes to give manager Ossie Ardiles a rare success against the Reds, as either manager or player.

THURSDAY 25th AUGUST 2011

Emmanuel Adebayor joins Spurs on a season-long loan from Manchester City. The controversial Togolese striker lost his place with the Blues after a reported fall-out with manager Roberto Mancini and was loaned out for much of the 2010/11 campaign to Real Madrid. When the Spanish giants didn't make the move permanent, he returned to City to find himself surplus to requirements. Harry Redknapp snaps up the talented striker claiming he can't fail to win. "If it doesn't work out, it's only a loan deal. If it does, great," he says.

MONDAY 26th AUGUST 1961

Terry Dyson hits a hat-trick in a north London derby as Arsenal are defeated 4-3 at White Hart Lane. Les Allen had put Spurs ahead, before Dyson got his first of the afternoon. The Gunners then score three times to give them a 3-2 lead going into the final 15 minutes and seemingly both points to boot. Dyson, however, was unwilling to give up on the game and scores his second and third to give his side the win and make him the first Tottenham player to have scored a hat-trick against Arsenal.

SATURDAY 27th AUGUST 1988

A mildly farcical situation arose when Spurs are refused a safety certificate for their opening game of the season at White Hart Lane, with Coventry City as the supposed visitors. The ground was being redeveloped at the time and work had continued throughout the summer. The club believed that, even with the work incomplete, they would still be passed fit to host the match. However, the safety inspectors' concerns could not be satisfied and embarrassingly, the match was postponed.

MONDAY 28th AUGUST 1950

Bolton Wanderers are defeated 4-2 at White Hart Lane as Spurs really begin to find their feet in the top flight. This was the club's second win of the season over the Trotters, with Len Duquemin (2), Eddie Baily and an own goal guaranteeing the win for the Lilywhites, who were looking to make an early impression on the league with their original 'push and run' style.

TUESDAY 28th AUGUST 1962

Paul Allen is born in Aveley, Essex. He would go on to make his Football League debut for West Ham United, aged just 17. It would take a fee of £400,000 to take him from his boyhood club to Spurs in 1985, where he went on to make 292 league appearances in eight seasons with the club. Allen would also pick up an FA Cup winners' medal in 1991 during a fine career in north London.

SUNDAY 28th AUGUST 2011

Bosnian international Edin Dzeko scores four as Manchester City win 5-1 in an opening home game massacre for Spurs. City, so fortunate to leave White Hart Lane just 12 months earlier following a dogged 0-0 draw, are a completely different proposition on this occasion, with Sergio Aguero, David Silva and Samir Nasri running amok. Dzeko scores City's first three goals in clinical fashion before Aguero makes it 4-0. Younes Kaboul pulls one back before Dzeko nets a stunning fourth in injury time to cap a disastrous day for Harry Redknapp's men which comes just a week after losing 3-0 to Manchester United.

THURSDAY 29th AUGUST 1974

Bill Nicholson announces his resignation from the role of manager following four straight defeats at the start of the season. One of the club's greatest managers cites a need to take time out from the sport, and had been dismayed by the violent actions of the club's fans in the previous season's Uefa Cup Final. No manager since has got near to matching his achievements at the club, with several periods of turmoil in the years after his departure.

SATURDAY 30th AUGUST 1919

Spurs started the post-war era in the Second Division following relegation in the final season before the conflict began. The team set their stall out early as they looked to get promoted at the first time of asking and they defeat Coventry City 5-0 away from home with a goal from Arthur Grimsdell and two apiece from Bert Bliss and Jimmy Chipperfield.

SATURDAY 31st AUGUST 2002

Spurs were still undefeated at this early point of the season and a win against Southampton sent them to the summit of the Premier League for a short period of time as their good form continues. With a real buzz around the club following the announcement Robbie Keane had joined from Leeds United, the Saints battle in vain at White Hart Lane as Tottenham's strike duo of Les Ferdinand and Teddy Sheringham cause all manner of problems all afternoon. Sheringham converts a last-minute penalty to guarantee the three points for Spurs and the visitors see a man dismissed, to add insult to injury.

WEDNESDAY 31st AUGUST 2011

England international Scott Parker signs for Spurs from West Ham for a fee of £5m, ending one of the transfer window's lengthier sagas. Parker, a boyhood Tottenham fan, is forced to hand in a transfer request as the Hammers battle in vain to keep hold of their talismanic midfielder but, eventually, the Irons' board accept the inevitable. The Football Writers' Player of the Year represents excellent value for Harry Redknapp who believes Parker will add verve and vigour to what had become a lacklustre engine room.

WEDNESDAY 31st AUGUST 2011

Peter Crouch signs for beaten FA Cup finalists Stoke City for a fee believed to be around £8m. Sunderland were also in for the England forward but Crouch elected to join Wilson Palacios at the Britannia Stadium believing that the ambitious Potters would offer him the greater chance of success. Whether his decision to quit White Hart Lane is proved to be a wise one remains to be seen.

SPURS
On This Day

SEPTEMBER

THURSDAY 1st SEPTEMBER 1908

Spurs' Football League debut comes in a home game in front of 20,000 spectators against Wolverhampton Wanderers. The fans were not disappointed as Spurs ran out 3-0 winners to prove their worth in the national ranks. The regally-named Vivian Woodward scores twice and Tom Morris grabs a third to ensure that the club get off to a flying start in their first match since being accepted into the Football League.

MONDAY 1st SEPTEMBER 2008

Roman Pavlyuchenko signs for £14m from Spartak Moscow. The striker had scored 89 goals in 141 matches for his previous club to become one of the hottest properties in the Russian league. The new arrival was not prolific in his first three seasons in England, scoring just 21 times in 70 appearances, as he was more often than not part of the squad's rotation system – i.e. on the bench a lot!

MONDAY 1st SEPTEMBER 2008

Striker Dimitar Berbatov leaves the club for a record £30.75m transfer fee to sign for Manchester United. The Bulgarian had arrived at White Hart Lane from German side Bayer Leverkusen in 2007. He went on to score 27 league goals for the club in 70 appearances. Berbatov also scored a penalty in Spurs' League Cup Final triumph over Chelsea but it was his sublime moments of skill that won him a legion of admirers at Tottenham. The striker who oozed class, but was sometimes accused on laziness, was also the subject of a bid from Manchester City on the same day, with the Blues reportedly offering more money, but he elected to head to Old Trafford instead.

WEDNESDAY 1st SEPTEMBER 2010

World Cup runner-up Rafael van der Vaart arrives from Real Madrid. The Dutchman was seen as surplus to requirements by the Spanish giants and Harry Redknapp jumps at the chance to sign him for what is a bargain fee of £8m. The mercurial midfielder made an instant impact in a Tottenham shirt, with some dazzling displays in both domestic and European competition accompanied by plenty of goals as Spurs attempted to consolidate their Champions League status.

SATURDAY 2nd SEPTEMBER 1939

The game that never was took place a day before the start of World War II was announced the following morning. Spurs took on West Bromwich Albion in the Midlands and managed to win the game 4-3 against the Baggies, but the match was wiped from the record books as the league calendar was cancelled with many of the players being called up to the armed forces. Johnny Morrison was the biggest loser, having scored a hat-trick in the victory with his treble effectively scratched from official statistics.

SATURDAY 3rd SEPTEMBER 1988

Paul Gascoigne is signed from his hometown club Newcastle United for £2m. It was not an easy task to convince the England midfielder to move to London, with Manchester United also interested in the playmaker. In a twist of fate he made his debut against his former club at St James' Park, with Gascoigne being booed throughout. Despite being two goals down at half-time, Spurs managed to salvage a point thanks to goals from Chris Waddle and Terry Fenwick to make it 2-2.

MONDAY 4th SEPTEMBER 1899

White Hart Lane plays host to its first game when Notts County are the opposition for a friendly match. At the time, the venue was known as 'The High Road Ground', and only got its current name after the end of World War II. The stands from their old ground at Northumberland Park were transferred to the new location, allowing 5,000 people to watch this match against the nation's oldest professional club. Fittingly, Spurs won 4-1 with David Copeland hitting a hat-trick and Tom Pratt getting the other.

SATURDAY 4th SEPTEMBER 1937

Les Allen is born in Dagenham. He signs for Spurs in 1959 from Chelsea. Allen was a prolific striker and formed a formidable partnership with Bobby Smith at White Hart Lane, notching 47 league goals for the club in 119 appearances before losing his place to Jimmy Greaves in 1965. Often playing second fiddle to the brilliant and prolific Greaves, Allen left, signing for QPR. He later managed the West London club, as well as Swindon Town.

TUESDAY 5th SEPTEMBER 1882

When a group of north London lads who were part of the Hotspur Cricket Club decided to form a football team, few could have known the outcome. This was the day that the club took its first subscriptions for members and is widely acknowledged as the birth date of the club, then known as Hotspur Football Club. They adopted the name Tottenham Hotspur two years later.

SUNDAY 6th SEPTEMBER 1998

Christian Gross arrives with a tube ticket in his hand, but left with nothing, having been sacked by Alan Sugar after only nine months in charge. The Swiss manager had been unpopular from day one, with both fans and players alike, and never looked like forming a successful side. Infamous excuses such as the 'grass being too long' ran thin with the Spurs faithful and he was never destined for an extended stay with the club, with David Pleat taking charge on his departure. A Gross error, perhaps? That's Christian, not Pleat.

SATURDAY 7th SEPTEMBER 1968

Spurs thrash Burnley 7-0 at White Hart Lane which is also the start of a three-month unbeaten period for the club. The goals included a brace from Cliff Jones, one each for Jimmy Robertson and Martin Chivers, with Jimmy Greaves netting a hat-trick with the Spurs marksman seemingly at the peak of his goalscoring powers. The emphatic win over the Clarets lifts Spurs up several places from fourth-bottom following an otherwise sluggish start.

SATURDAY 8th SEPTEMBER 1990

Paul Gascoigne spent the early part of the season proving that he was one of the best players in Europe with his hat-trick against Derby County being one of his finest performances for the club. The Tottenham fans were left drooling as Gascoigne ran the game, and won it almost single-handedly with a mixture of skill, guile, vision and controlled aggression. The 3-0 win over the Rams put unbeaten Spurs into fourth place in Division One, just four points adrift of leaders Liverpool.

JIMMY GREAVES HIT A HAT-TRICK IN A 7-0 WIN OVER BURNLEY IN SEPTEMBER 1968.

SATURDAY 9th SEPTEMBER 1967

Spurs' 2,000th league match was played at White Hart Lane with Sheffield Wednesday providing the opposition. The team celebrated by defeating the men from South Yorkshire 2-1. Alan Gilzean and Frank Saul were the men on target, as Spurs took the points in a close encounter to make it a successful afternoon's work.

SATURDAY 10th SEPTEMBER 1960

Spurs notch an impressive 100% record from the first seven games of the season, made all the sweeter with their first win at Highbury in four years. It was a sign of things to come in the double-winning season. Frank Saul, Terry Dyson and Les Allen made the difference in this north London derby by scoring Tottenham's goals in a 3-2 victory that already sees them two points clear of nearest challengers Sheffield Wednesday at the top of Division One.

WEDNESDAY 11th SEPTEMBER 1974

The feeling around Bill Nicholson's departure from White Hart Lane was summed up by his final game in charge as his team lose 4-0 at home against Middlesbrough in the League Cup. He had handed in his resignation the previous week, but agreed to stay on until a replacement was found. The players seemed dispirited by his imminent loss, couldn't raise their game and were never better than second best against the Teessiders.

SATURDAY 12th SEPTEMBER 1959

Spurs performed a demolition of Manchester United at Old Trafford that had rarely been seen before, or since for that matter. Tottenham scored five, with United unable to cope with the slick style and flair of a team playing almost unstoppable attacking football. The visitors raced into a three-goal lead thanks to David Dunmore, Bobby Smith and Tommy Harmer, with the Red Devils pulling one back before half-time. In the days before substitutes, Spurs started the second period a man down, as Smith received treatment for a facial injury, but returned to the pitch to add a fourth, before Dave Mackay netted the fifth. Ten men... we only need ten men...

WEDNESDAY 13th SEPTEMBER 1961

Spurs turn around a dire situation to come home with a decent result after a brutal welcome to the European Cup when they took on Gornik Zabrze in the first round. The Poles took a four-goal lead, but were reduced to nine men due to some robust challenges, and due to the lack of replacements at the time. Spurs salvaged something from the game, as Cliff Jones and Terry Dyson gave them something to build on in the second leg, also giving the Lilywhites two vital away goals.

SATURDAY 14th SEPTEMBER 1974

Former Arsenal player Terry Neill is appointed manager – much to the dismay of the Spurs fans – as the club's board choose to ignore Bill Nicholson's recommendation to hire Danny Blanchflower and Johnny Giles as the managerial team. However, the team respond well to the appointment as they beat West Ham United 2-1, with goals coming from Mike England and Martin Chivers.

SATURDAY 15th SEPTEMBER 1951

Spurs travel to the Potteries in confident mood with opponents Stoke City firmly rooted to the bottom of the table. The Lilywhites were right to be optimistic as they despatched the Potters 6-1 at the Victoria Ground. Sid McClellan and Les Bennett net early on with Alf Ramsey adding a penalty to give them a three-goal lead. Sonny Walters and Les Medley, the latter scoring twice, removed any vague lingering doubt that the hosts could mount some miraculous comeback, though they do manage a late consolation. The win sees Spurs climb to fourth, just two points off the summit as their bid to retain the title begins to ignite.

WEDNESDAY 16th SEPTEMBER 1981

Spurs return to action in Europe's premier competition with a game against the thrilling Total Football philosophy of Ajax. Many thought Spurs would struggle against the slickness of the Dutchmen, but the Lilywhites leave Amsterdam with an impressive 3-1 win. Ricky Villa nets the first, before two goals from Mark Falco confirms Tottenham's superiority on the night, proving English football is still as vibrant as ever.

MONDAY 17th SEPTEMBER 1956

Floodlights were still in their infancy, with their novelty meaning that the Scottish and English FAs created a competition to get full value out of them. Spurs took on Hibernian in Edinburgh in the Anglo-Scottish Floodlight Cup. It wasn't an official tournament, as no bodies had ratified it, forcing the matches to be played as friendlies. Spurs dominated the match in the Scottish capital from start to finish, running out 5-1 winners, with goals from Bobby Smith (2), Danny Blanchflower, Tommy Harmer and Terry Dyson.

SATURDAY 18th SEPTEMBER 1993

Joe Royle's Oldham Athletic are demolished at White Hart Lane, conceding five goals without reply. Steve Sedgley scores a quarter of his Spurs career goals in this game by netting twice. In-form striker Teddy Sheringham notches his seventh goal in the first eight games of the season. Spurs were three goals to the good at half-time, but didn't rest on their laurels, netting twice more in the second period thanks to strikes from Jason Dozzell and Gordon Durie. The win puts Tottenham into fifth, just two points behind Premier League leaders Manchester United.

WEDNESDAY 19th SEPTEMBER 1973

Spurs travel to Switzerland to take on Grasshoppers Zurich in the first round of the Uefa Cup. Despite winning 5-1, many saw goalkeeper Pat Jennings as the star performer on the night. Martin Chivers and Ray Evans set Spurs on their way, before Grasshoppers pulled one back. Spurs were re-invigorated after this with Chivers scoring his second of the game, with Alan Gilzean adding some gloss to the result with two late goals, though Jennings kept a lively Zurich attack at bay at crucial moments of the game to fully play his part in the victory.

SUNDAY 19th SEPTEMBER 2004

A date that Spurs have only lost once on in 21 games sees the Lilywhites earn a valuable 0-0 draw away to Chelsea. The point lifts Tottenham into fifth while Chelsea, who hit the woodwork and see Paul Robinson make several fine saves, remain in second.

WEDNESDAY 20th SEPTEMBER 1961

Trailing 4-2 from the first match against a slick, if overly-physical, Gornik Zabzre side, Tottenham turn on the style on an incredible night at White Hart Lane. Ninety minutes, and eight goals later, Spurs had waltzed into the next round of the European Cup after an 8-1 demolition of the Poles. Danny Blanchflower converted a penalty, before Cliff Jones struck a quick-fire 17-minute hat-trick prior to half-time. Zabrze pulling one back didn't perturb Spurs as they net four more times, with Bobby Smith scoring either side of half-time, followed by Terry Dyson and Johnny White finishing the scoring to win 10-5 on aggregate – not bad considering it had been 4-0 to Gornik at one point in the first leg!

WEDNESDAY 21st SEPTEMBER 1994

An annihilation of Watford at Vicarage Road sets Spurs on the League Cup trail once again. Ossie Ardiles was taking no chances, with Ilie Dumitrescu, Teddy Sheringham and Darren Anderton all getting their names on the score-sheet. Their achievements were all eclipsed by Jurgen Klinsmann's stunning hat-trick in the superbly entertaining 6-3 victory.

WEDNESDAY 22nd SEPTEMBER 1971

The Anglo-Italian League Cup Winners' Cup wasn't the most highly respected of competitions, but it allowed Spurs to take on Torino over two legs at the start of the season and was seen by many as more of an educational opportunity for players getting used to European opposition. Spurs led by a single goal from the first leg, and dominated the second at White Hart Lane, with the ever-reliable duo of Martin Chivers and Alan Gilzean making sure the trophy stayed in north London.

SATURDAY 23rd SEPTEMBER 1989

Following a slow start to his Spurs career, Gary Lineker finally found his feet in a league game at Carrow Road. The striker nets his first goal for the club, scoring the second of Tottenham's goals in a 2-2 draw with the Canaries who have now drawn all four home games. Paul Gascoigne scores the first, with his England team-mate guaranteeing a point for Spurs who remain second-bottom of Division One.

SATURDAY 24th SEPTEMBER 1983

Glenn Hoddle scores one of the finest goals of his career as he chips the Watford goalkeeper in this 3-2 away win at Vicarage Road. The midfielder had a fine all-round game, with his strike providing added gloss. Substitute Steve Archibald scores Spurs' second with Chris Hughton firing in the third to ensure the points head back to White Hart Lane.

MONDAY 25th SEPTEMBER 1995

Spurs travelled across London to face Queens Park Rangers for a game shown live on television. The home side went two goals ahead, before Spurs got into their stride with Teddy Sheringham reducing the deficit and Jason Dozzell levelling with 20 minutes left on the clock. The scores were equal for only a few minutes, as Sheringham popped up again to score the winner to earn the three points.

SATURDAY 26th SEPTEMBER 1998

The on-field action was as intriguing as the happenings away from the pitch when Leeds United arrived at White Hart Lane with the Yorkshire club's manager George Graham the shock favourite to take the vacant manager's job at Spurs. The former Arsenal boss was an unpopular choice for the Spurs fans, many of whom made their opinion known throughout the game. From the first whistle it was a pulsating game with the teams sharing six goals. Ramon Vega, Steffen Iversen and Sol Campbell were the men to score for the home side, as Spurs confirmed a point late on. Graham was appointed as the club's new manager later that week.

WEDNESDAY 27th SEPTEMBER 1967

Spurs confirm their passage to the next round of the European Cup Winners' Cup by defeating Hajduk Split 4-3 at White Hart Lane. Admittedly, Spurs held a two-goal lead from the first leg, but it was important that they got the job done with minimal fuss and things couldn't have gone better – initially. The Lilywhites were soon 3-0 up with Jimmy Robertson, Alan Gilzean and Terry Venables all getting on the score-sheet. Split pulled two goals back, but hopes of a historical comeback were shattered when Robertson doubled his tally for the night, making a late penalty from the visitors no more than a consolation.

TUESDAY 28th SEPTEMBER 1971

Spurs scored 15 times in the two games they played against Keflavik of Iceland in the Uefa Cup. Six came in the first leg and a demoralised outfit arrived in England to merely carry out the formalities of a second match. Spurs hit nine as the gulf in class became more painful for the punch-drunk visitors. Martin Chivers nets a typical poacher's hat-trick, with the other goals coming from Alan Gilzean (2), Steve Perryman, Ralph Coates, Cyril Knowles and Phil Holder.

SATURDAY 29th SEPTEMBER 2012

Andre Villas-Boas becomes the first Tottenham manager to win at Old Trafford in 23 years, after his side beat Manchester United 3-2 in a swashbuckling victory over the Reds. Johnny Evans' own goal after two minutes and Gareth Bale's brilliant solo strike thirty minutes later gave Spurs a 2-0 lead at the break but a crazy three-minute period just after the break sees Nani and Kagawa's goals sandwiched by Clint Dempsey's 52nd minute winner. Though they have to hold out for a further 37 minutes plus five minutes of 'Fergie time', there are no more goals.

SATURDAY 30th SEPTEMBER 1882

Hotspur FC took to the pitch for the first time as they faced Radicals FC. It wasn't the best start for the newly formed club as they lost 2-0. This was the club's first recorded match and is seen to have taken place between a collection of schoolboys. But, as far as the historians are concerned, it was the start of what is now Tottenham Hotspur.

SATURDAY 30th SEPTEMBER 2000

Two goals from Sergei Rebrov and a rare Chris Perry goal see Spurs hit three goals at Elland Road – yet still lose to a Mark Viduka-inspired Leeds United 4-3. The Australian striker scores twice, as does Alan Smith, as Tottenham throw a 1-0 half-time lead away in a second-half onslaught.

SPURS
On This Day

OCTOBER

TUESDAY 1st OCTOBER 1912

Notts County's first four-figure transfer fee is received when Jimmy Cantrell moves to Spurs. Cantrell began life as a defender at Meadow Lane, converting to a striker to great effect and ending top scorer for three out of the five years he was with the Magpies. Cantrell's goals continued to flow in a Spurs shirt and during his 11 years at White Hart Lane, he bagged 84 goals in 174 appearances.

SATURDAY 1st OCTOBER 1966

Spurs come out on top in a seven-goal thriller with Fulham at Craven Cottage. Jimmy Greaves nets in his seventh successive game when he scores Spurs' second after Jimmy Robertson had got the first. Alan Gilzean's first away goal for 18 months and Terry Venables' first for the club were enough to take the points back from west to north London.

WEDNESDAY 2nd OCTOBER 1991

Spurs overturn a one-goal deficit from the first leg against Hajduk Split in the European Cup Winners' Cup to advance to the next round. Young defender David Tuttle scores his only goal for the club, on his European debut, with Gordon Durie bagging the crucial second that guaranteed Spurs' progression.

SATURDAY 3rd OCTOBER 1908

A scoreless draw against second-place Derby County at White Hart Lane is the first point that Spurs had dropped at home in their fledgling Football League career. The club had won their three previous home games in Division Two, but were unable to find the back of the net in this encounter. The point keeps Spurs in seventh in the table, just four points off the top.

TUESDAY 4th OCTOBER 1977

Having started the season undefeated, third-place Spurs are disappointed to leave Boothferry Park on the wrong end of a 2-0 loss, with the Lilywhites looking to return to the top flight at the first attempt. Hull put an early dent in the visitors' promotion hopes by shutting out an impressive Spurs attack – inflicting the first defeat on Tottenham in nine matches.

SATURDAY 5th OCTOBER 1974

Tottenham's bid to climb away from the foot of the table is thwarted as Burnley take both points at White Hart Lane and leave the Lilywhites just one place off the bottom. The only consolation for Spurs fans is that Arsenal are the team propping the division up! Mike England and John Pratt scored for the hosts on the day, but it wasn't enough to stop the Clarets as they inflicted a 3-2 defeat to continue Spurs' worrying form.

SATURDAY 6th OCTOBER 1962

The Spurs faithful were understandably delirious when the Lilywhites go three goals ahead early on against Arsenal in the north London derby. However, it wasn't to be as the Gunners eventually manage to earn a point in a pulsating 4-4 draw. Spurs' goals were scored by Dave Mackay, and Johnny White, whilst Cliff Jones nets twice. It won't be the last 4-4 draw between these two great rivals, either.

SATURDAY 7th OCTOBER 1972

Stoke head back north feeling hard done by following a narrow 4-3 defeat at White Hart Lane. The Potters did their best to nullify the Spurs attack but are still picked off at ease. John Pratt's brace is the platform for Spurs' win, with Alan Gilzean and Ralph Coates the others to get their names on the score-sheet.

SATURDAY 8th OCTOBER 1932

Spurs had started the season in worrying fashion but a 6-2 win at Preston North End was to be the kick-start that the team desperately needed. Davie Colquhoun, Taffy O'Callaghan, George Hunt and George Greenfield got a goal each, with Willie Evans scoring two. The team would then go on a 12-game unbeaten streak.

SATURDAY 8th OCTOBER 1994

A disappointing home game with QPR ends 1-1. Though Spurs have won three of their four games on the road this season, it was only the fourth home point out of a possible 15.

TUESDAY 9th OCTOBER 2001

Tranmere Rovers are the opposition for a third-round League Cup tie at Prenton Park and the Wirral outfit are easily despatched by a clinical Tottenham side who score four without reply. The game wasn't taken lightly by the regular Wembley visitors – as the trend was with the League Cup at the time. The quality of the starting XI is illustrated in the four scorers on the night: Teddy Sheringham, Darren Anderton, Gus Poyet and Sergei Rebrov.

MONDAY 10th OCTOBER 1960

Spurs' 100% record ends as Manchester City earn a 1-1 draw at White Hart Lane. The team had previously won the first 11 outings of the campaign but faced stern resistance from the Blues. Unusually played on a Monday, along with a clutch of League Cup ties, Bobby Smith puts Spurs ahead, but a determined City side battle their way back into the game through a Colbridge equaliser. The statistics indicate that Spurs should have had more after clocking up an incredible 39 shots, compared to the away side's nine, all watched by a crowd close to 60,000.

SATURDAY 11th OCTOBER 1958

Bill Nicholson was probably hoping for a calm, collected opening to his managerial career, but instead saw his new Spurs side win 10-4 against Everton – not that he or anyone else was complaining! Six of Spurs' goals were scored before half-time as Nicholson's team seemed intent on impressing their new manager. Bobby Smith took the headlines as he scored four, though he was ably supported by his colleagues. Alf Stokes scored two while there were one each for Johnny Ryden, Terry Medwin, Tommy Harmer and George Robb. Little did Spurs fans know that this was just the beginning of what would be a golden era under Nicholson. He goes on to guide the Lilywhites through the most successful period in the club's history.

WEDNESDAY 11th OCTOBER 1972

Middlesbrough force another replay in the League Cup third-round rematch at White Hart Lane. Despite 90 minutes of normal time, and another 30 minutes of extra time, Spurs can't find a goal against the Division Two Teessiders.

SATURDAY 12th OCTOBER 1957

After a poor start to the season the Spurs fans were fearful of a heavy defeat to Arsenal but these fears prove unfounded as the Lilywhites turn on the style to win 3-1 at White Hart Lane. The hosts go three goals ahead thanks to Bobby Smith's opener, and two from Terry Medwin, with the Gunners only managing a penalty in response.

SUNDAY 12th OCTOBER 1980

Ledley King is born in Stepney. He would go on to be a powerful defender for Spurs whose career would be continually blighted by knee injuries. King signed professional forms in 1998, and made his debut against Liverpool the following year. In the early part of his career he was repeatedly used as a central midfielder, but found his best position to be in the back four. He was appointed as the club captain in 2004, but was unable to lead the side on many occasions due to continuing fitness issues. King had earned 21 international caps up to August 2011.

SATURDAY 13th OCTOBER 1894

Spurs play their first FA Cup tie, when they face West Herts – who will later become Watford – at home. Peter Hunter wrote his name into the club's history books as he scored Spurs' first goal in the competition. Donald Goodall scored twice more for Tottenham as they edged the game 3-2.

SATURDAY 14th OCTOBER 1967

Spurs see off Coventry City 3-2 at Highfield Road in this top-flight encounter, the first between the clubs for 18 years. The talismanic Jimmy Greaves was once again the hero as he scores twice with Cliff Jones ensuring that Spurs left with both points, securing a third away victory of the season.

SATURDAY 14th OCTOBER 2006

Juan Pablo Angel's 76th-minute own goal looks to have given Spurs all three points in this Villa Park Premier League battle, but Gareth Barry levels for the hosts just five minutes later to earn a share of the spoils.

TUESDAY 15th OCTOBER 1963

Incredibly, Spurs and Arsenal produce their second 4-4 draw in three meetings in one of the greatest north London derbies of all time. With a 3-2 win for the Lilywhites sandwiched in between, it meant the two clubs had shared 21 goals in just three meetings – an amazing statistic. Spurs looked like they were heading for the victory when they went in at half-time winning 4-2 thanks to Jimmy Greaves' strike, Bobby Smith's double and Dave Mackay's effort. The visitors still led with only moments remaining, but Arsenal came back from the dead to snatch a draw.

SATURDAY 16th OCTOBER 1965

Jimmy Greaves scores the goal of the season in a 5-1 win over Manchester United at White Hart Lane. The striker gets hold of the ball in his own half and weaves his way through the opposition's rearguard before rounding the goalkeeper and calmly tapping home. The other scorers that day were Jimmy Robertson, Alan Gilzean, Eddie Clayton and Neil Johnson.

SATURDAY 17th OCTOBER 1885

Spurs have their first competitive outing in a London Association Cup tie against St Albans. Six of the club's founding members were on the team-sheet as the side ran out 5-2 victors to confirm their progression to the next round, where the cup adventure that season ends. However, it was still a pleasant start to life in knockout competitions that the Lilywhites would develop a great thirst for in the years to come.

WEDNESDAY 18th OCTOBER 1989

Having lost six clashes with Arsenal in a row, Spurs end their north London derby jinx as Terry Venables' men run out 2-1 winners at White Hart Lane. Both of Tottenham's goals are scored in a five-minute period in the first half as Tony Adams concedes two free kicks that are smartly despatched by Vinny Samways and Paul Walsh. Arsenal pull a goal back in the second half, but Spurs come away with the points thanks in no small part to the terrific display by goalkeeper Erik Thorstvedt.

ERIK THORSTVEDT HELPED SPURS END A WINLESS STREAK AGAINST ARSENAL IN OCTOBER 1989.

WEDNESDAY 19th OCTOBER 1983

One of the all-time world greats, Johan Cruyff, comes to White Hart Lane as Spurs face Feyenoord in the Uefa Cup. However, it is Spurs' own midfield genius, Glenn Hoddle, who steals the show as Spurs win 4-2. The match was effectively over by half-time with Spurs four goals ahead largely due to the influence of Hoddle, no doubt inspired by one of his boyhood heroes. Steve Archibald and Tony Galvin score twice each with the England midfielder pivotal in setting two goals up on the night.

SATURDAY 19th OCTOBER 1991

Irish striker Niall Quinn's solitary goal gives Manchester City a rare 1-0 win at White Hart Lane. The victory is the Blues' third successive win on the road – a contrast to the form at Maine Road where Peter Reid's side have lost three on the bounce. Despite the home wobbles, City move up to third, six points behind leaders Manchester United, while Spurs count the cost of a third defeat in four home games, dropping to 13th as a result. Interestingly, though Spurs lose the return game at Maine Road by the same score, City will only win one of the next 13 meetings thereafter.

WEDNESDAY 20th OCTOBER 1982

A depleted Spurs side come up against Bayern Munich in the European Cup Winners' Cup, gaining a creditable 1-1 home draw, considering the number of players absent. Spurs take the lead early on thanks to Steve Archibald, but couldn't gain any momentum and were pegged back by an important away goal to hand the advantage to the Germans.

SATURDAY 21st OCTOBER 2000

Spurs welcome Derby County to north London as they look to get their season back on track after a streak of four winless matches. Oyvind Leonhardsen scores after five minutes to boost Spurs' chances of ending the poor run before the Rams equalise. A Stephen Carr wonder strike regains the lead for Tottenham on the stroke of half-time and a 3-1 win is confirmed when Norwegian Leonhardsen grabs his second late on.

SATURDAY 22nd OCTOBER 1977

Colin Lee scores four goals on an incredible Spurs debut – just two days after signing from Torquay United. The victims of the nine-goal rout are Bristol Rovers in their first ever league visit – and the *Match of the Day* cameras are at White Hart Lane to record everything for posterity. Rovers' only previous visit to Spurs had ended in a 6-1 defeat in 1921 so they should have known what was in store! At the end of the season, Spurs win promotion back to the top flight on goal difference – coincidentally the margin is nine! Ian Moores hit a hat-trick of his own, with Peter Taylor and Glenn Hoddle netting a goal each. The return game against the Pirates was a closer affair, with Spurs just edging a 3-2 win.

SATURDAY 23rd OCTOBER 1938

Alan Gilzean is born in Coupar Angus, Scotland. On a goals-per-game ratio for Scotland, Alan Gilzean's strike record is up among the very best and he is also a Tottenham legend in every sense of the word with 93 goals in 343 appearances. Better than one every two games for his country, Gilzean made his debut in a 6-1 win over Norway in 1963 though, ironically, he was not among the scorers that day. Then a Dundee player, he scored his first Scotland goal in a 1-0 win over the English at Hampden Park in 1964 before taking part in a fundraising game for a Scotland select side against Tottenham Hotspur following the death of fellow Scot John White. Gilzean scored two goals at White Hart Lane during that game – and promptly found himself a new club south of the border as Spurs snapped up the prolific forward for £72,500. Gilzean soon forged an excellent strike partnership with Jimmy Greaves and continued to represent his country with great effect, scoring twice on four different occasions, most memorably away to West Germany in 1964. Gilzean's final appearance for his country was in April 1971 against Portugal and he retired from club football three years later.

SATURDAY 23rd OCTOBER 1967

Spurs pick up a useful point away to Newcastle United in a Division One clash at St James' Park. Though the 0-0 draw is a fair result, it highlights the Lilywhites' poor form on the road which sees them remain winless away from White Hart Lane.

WEDNESDAY 23rd OCTOBER 1991

Spurs were making good progress in the European Cup Winners' Cup, on their return to action on the continent. English clubs were once again eligible to take part in European competition following the Heysel disaster six years earlier and Porto arrive in London hoping to halt the Lilywhites in their tracks, but leave having lost 3-1 thanks to a brace from Gary Lineker and another goal from Gordon Durie.

MONDAY 24th OCTOBER 1921

Ted Ditchburn is born in Gillingham. The goalkeeper went on to become one of the club's great custodians. He spent some time on the ground staff, prior to signing professional forms in 1939. Ditchburn made his debut in a war-time league game against Chelsea. Following the war, he enjoyed a period of 247 consecutive appearances for Spurs over six years.

WEDNESDAY 24th OCTOBER 1962

High-scoring games were a regular occurrence at White Hart Lane around this period and Manchester United become the latest victims of free-scoring Spurs in a 6-2 drubbing. A Jimmy Greaves strike and two from Terry Medwin set Spurs up for the win before half-time with the prolific Greaves netting twice more in the second half and Cliff Jones completing the scoring before United got two consolation goals.

WEDNESDAY 25th OCTOBER 1989

Spurs get the better of Manchester United at Old Trafford as the north Londoners score three without reply in a rare Old Trafford triumph. Gary Lineker, Vinny Samways and Nayim make the difference on the night as Spurs ease to victory in the League Cup third round.

WEDNESDAY 26th OCTOBER 1994

Ossie Ardiles had been a great club servant, as both a player and manager, but his footballing philosophy was no longer working and with the fans and directors frustrated at recent defeats, his fate was sealed in an embarrassing League Cup defeat at Notts County. Unsurprisingly, Ardiles did not manage to see out another seven days in charge and was relieved of his duties soon after this 3-0 third-round loss to a side a division below.

GARY LINEKER GRABBED A BRACE AGAINST PORTO IN OCTOBER 1991.

SUNDAY 26th OCTOBER 2008

Harry Redknapp is appointed manager of Tottenham Hotspur. When Redknapp first arrived, Spurs only had two points from the opening eight matches. The club's form soon picked up and the Lilywhites easily avoided relegation. In Redknapp's first full season in charge, the team finished fourth with 70 points, meaning they had qualified for the Champions League play-offs. Thanks to this fantastic performance in the Premier League, Redknapp won the Manager of the Year award, too. The man from Poplar took Spurs into their first campaign in Europe's premier competition, eventually going out to Real Madrid in the quarter-finals.

SATURDAY 27th OCTOBER 1928

Cecil Poynton is the only Spurs player to be sent off for 37 years when he is dismissed in a league game at Stoke. Full-back Poynton later made up for his misdemeanour, enjoying a 50-year association with the club in a variety of roles including player, coach and physio. Spurs lost 2-0 to the Potters on the day, but it wouldn't be until 1965 when another player is shown a red card.

SUNDAY 27th OCTOBER 1957

Glenn Hoddle is born in Hayes. The gifted playmaker arrived at Spurs on schoolboy forms in April 1974, making his first-team debut the following year at the age of 17. He went on to play 377 times for Spurs in 12 years, before moving to French outfit, Monaco. Away from the pitch he teamed up with Chris Waddle to sing the embarrassing 'Diamond Lights', appearing on *Top of the Pops* with his mullet-wearing team-mate – the song somehow made number 12 in the UK charts. Hoddle made 51 appearances for England, seen as one of the players of his generation. He returned to White Hart Lane in 2001 to take over as manager, but his time in charge was a pale shadow of his playing career.

SATURDAY 27th OCTOBER 1973

Spurs continue to struggle as Newcastle United leave White Hart Lane with a 2-0 victory. The defeat leaves the Lilywhites precariously placed above the relegation zone, though with plenty of time to pull clear.

SATURDAY 27th OCTOBER 2007

Spaniard Juande Ramos is appointed manager. The former Seville coach arrived with a big reputation having won the Uefa Cup and European Super Cup whilst in charge at the Andalusian club. Ramos had only been in charge for four months when he took his side to Wembley to take on Chelsea in the League Cup Final, which Spurs won. Unfortunately, Ramos couldn't build on this success, and led the team to their worst start to a league season, and was dismissed only a year after taking charge. He has since gone on to manage Real Madrid and CSKA Moscow.

SATURDAY 28th OCTOBER 1972

England striker Martin Peters scored all four of Spurs' goals at Old Trafford in a 4-1 win over Manchester United. It was the club's first points in ten trips to Old Trafford and was a satisfying victory, even if it came against one of the weaker United teams of recent decades.

SATURDAY 29th OCTOBER 1960

Spurs win 4-3 at St James' Park in front of a season-high crowd for Newcastle United. Despite Maurice Norman's first-half goal, Spurs find themselves behind at the interval. A galvanised Tottenham come out for the second period, with Johnny White and Cliff Jones giving them an advantage. However, Newcastle restore parity, but Spurs would not be denied as Bobby Smith headed home an 87th-minute winner.

WEDNESDAY 29th OCTOBER 2008

A frenetic north London derby ends 4-4 at the Emirates thanks to a last-gasp equaliser from Aaron Lennon. It was former Arsenal man David Bentley who opened the scoring after 13 minutes with an audacious strike from distance. The home side then fought back, scoring three unanswered goals against their rivals to move into a 3-1 lead, before Darren Bent pulled one back. Arsenal then recovered their two-goal advantage only a minute later, leaving Spurs with it all to do. Spurs scored two in the final moments of the game to clinch an unlikely point as first Jermaine Jenas netted, before Lennon struck in injury-time in Harry Redknapp's first game in charge.

MONDAY 30th OCTOBER 1972

Spurs defeat Middlesbrough after extra time of their second replay in the third round of the League Cup. In the days of replays, sides played until one succumbed to the other, rather than a penalty shoot-out. On this occasion the teams went in to the additional 30 minutes with one goal each. Spurs' goal comes from Martin Peters. With the game heading to yet another encounter between the sides, Alan Gilzean scores the winner to ensure the match finishes on the night.

SUNDAY 30th OCTOBER 2010

Nemanja Vidic, and a controversial late second from Nani, ensures Spurs' 21-year wait for a win at Old Trafford continues with a 2-0 defeat.

WEDNESDAY 31st OCTOBER 1962

Like any game between English and Scottish sides, when Spurs took on Rangers in the European Cup Winners' Cup, it was dubbed 'The Battle of Britain'. The first leg was a hard-fought affair with Johnny White running the show against his countrymen as Spurs won 5-2. White scored twice, with Les Allen, Maurice Norman and an own goal giving Spurs a commanding three-goal advantage as they headed to Ibrox for the return match.

TUESDAY 31st OCTOBER 2000

A real Halloween horror at White Hart Lane as Spurs are dumped out of the League Cup by Birmingham City. The visitors establish a 3-0 first-half lead courtesy of two goals from Dele Adebola, and a killer third from Mark Burchill on the stroke of half-time. A penalty from Darren Anderton on the hour gives the majority of the 27,096 crowd hope, but Blues hang on for a deserved victory.

WEDNESDAY 31st OCTOBER 2007

A goal in each half from Robbie Keane and Pascal Chimbonda put Spurs through to the next round of the League Cup against Blackpool. Though the Championship side put up a decent display, the Lilywhites' passage is never in any real danger in front of a crowd in excess of 32,000.

SPURS
On This Day

NOVEMBER

WEDNESDAY 1st NOVEMBER 1893

Ernie Payne's 50p boots cause a rumpus. Payne was at the centre of a scandal that saw Spurs suspended from action for two weeks by the London FA who took the matter very seriously indeed. The player had been brought in from Fulham, but the West Londoners claimed they still held his registration and that he had been acquired illegally by Spurs. It was alleged that Spurs had offered the player 50p to purchase a new pair of boots, which was seen as an unfair inducement, as the club were found guilty and punished. Still, Payne had the best boots at the club so all was not lost!

TUESDAY 2nd NOVEMBER 1971

Spurs progress to the next round of the Uefa Cup thanks to a single goal at White Hart Lane in a two-legged affair against French outfit Nantes. Martin Peters was the man who made the difference over the 180 minutes with a typical poacher's goal in the first half. The only other point of interest was when Nantes managed to have 12 players on the pitch for a short period due to confusion over a substitution – and still couldn't score!

TUESDAY 2nd NOVEMBER 2010

Gareth Bale turns in an imperious display as Spurs beat European champions Inter Milan 3-1 on a glorious night at White Hart Lane. Though Bale scored a hat-trick in the first meeting between the two teams at the San Siro – and ended on the losing team – this time he doesn't score but instead runs the Italians' defence ragged with a superb individual display. Rafael van der Vaart puts Spurs on their way with a goal after 18 minutes and Bale sets up Peter Crouch to make it 2-0 early in the second half. Bale torments Brazilian right-back Maicon to the point of embarrassment and the home fans' chant of 'Taxi for Maicon!' brings light relief to the capacity crowd. Samuel Eto'o pulls one back on 81 minutes before Bale sets up Roman Pavlyuchenko in the last minute to make it 3-1. Many believe it is Bale's two stellar performances against Inter alone that are the reason he is later voted PFA Player of the Year.

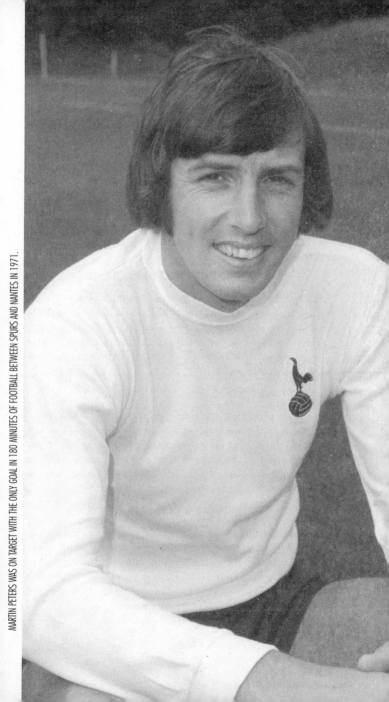

SATURDAY 3rd NOVEMBER 1951

Spurs see off Wolverhampton Wanderers in a 4-2 win at White Hart Lane. It was the team's sixth win in eight games, as they looked to retain the league title. The crucial goals came from Alf Ramsey, Sonny Walters, Les Bennett and Len Duquemin in front of 61,000-plus fans.

THURSDAY 4th NOVEMBER 1999

Late, late drama as Tottenham crash out of the Uefa Cup against Kaiserslautern, who win 2-0 in the second leg of the cup clash in Germany. Spurs had won the first game by a single goal and for much of the game seemed to be heading through, only to lose concentration in the dying seconds as the Germans score twice in injury time to go through.

SATURDAY 5th NOVEMBER 1960

Spurs begin the season with an unbeaten run of 16 games, including this 5-1 thrashing of Fulham at White Hart Lane. Les Allen and Cliff Jones start the rout with two goals in the first half, but the Cottagers reduce the arrears early in the second period only for Spurs' backlash to shift back up a gear as Jones scores his second. Johnny White and Allen kill the game off.

WEDNESDAY 6th NOVEMBER 2002

A desperate performance at Turf Moor sees Spurs knocked out of the League Cup at the hands of Burnley. Gus Poyet had given the Lilywhites the lead, but there seems no desire to put the game to bed from the somewhat casual visitors allowing the Clarets back into the tie as they equalise. Burnley continued to dominate thereafter, scoring the winner in the second half to give them a 2-1 victory.

THURSDAY 6th NOVEMBER 2008

Young midfielder John Bostock becomes the club's youngest player at 16 and 295 days, when he makes a late substitute appearance against Dinamo Zagreb in the Uefa Cup, with Tottenham easing to a 4-0 win. Bostock arrived from Crystal Palace after making only four first-team appearances for the south Londoners. In his first three years with Spurs he failed to make a single league appearance.

SUNDAY 7th NOVEMBER 1999

Spurs blitz Arsenal in the first 20 minutes of the north London derby with the team in white going two goals ahead. Steffen Iversen and Tim Sherwood score the goals early on, but Arsenal come back into the game with a goal before half-time. The Gunners self-destruct after the interval with Martin Keown and Freddie Ljungberg red carded, making Spurs' job of keeping the remaining nine players out a lot simpler. The score ends 2-1 to the hosts.

SATURDAY 8th NOVEMBER 1997

Liverpool thrash Spurs by scoring four goals without reply at Anfield. The first half ends goalless, but it only took two minutes of the second period for Liverpool to open the scoring when Steve McManaman nets the opener. Strikes from Oyvind Leonhardsen, Jamie Redknapp and Michael Owen would confirm the points for the home side in front of over 38,000 fans. The defeat leaves Spurs in 16th place while Liverpool move up to sixth.

SATURDAY 8th NOVEMBER 2003

Spurs lose at Highbury despite taking an early lead. Darren Anderton scores within five minutes, but his side is unable to build on the early advantage and succumb to Arsenal in the second half when the Gunners score twice.

MONDAY 8th NOVEMBER 2004

Dutchman Martin Jol is appointed head coach, replacing Jacques Santini. He had been the Frenchman's assistant during his disastrous spell in charge, but was promoted on his departure. In the 2005/06 campaign he took Spurs to fifth for successive seasons, but the board decided that this wasn't sufficient and Jol was sent packing in October 2007, allegedly sacked during a 2-1 defeat to Getafe.

WEDNESDAY 9th NOVEMBER 1988

Spurs travel to Ewood Park for a League Cup replay on a clichéd wet Wednesday in November. After a goalless draw at White Hart Lane, the Lilywhites manage to secure a 2-1 win at the expense of Blackburn Rovers with Mitchell Thomas and Paul Stewart scoring the goals that see Spurs home.

TUESDAY 10th NOVEMBER 1998

Spurs record an impressive 3-1 win at Anfield in the League Cup. Things start well with a goal from Steffen Iversen after just two minutes giving the visitors a solid platform to build on. John Scales and Allan Nielsen put Spurs three up with Liverpool getting a consolation goal.

TUESDAY 11th NOVEMBER 1964

A memorial match takes place in honour of the Spurs favourite Johnny White who is struck and killed by lightning while playing golf. The fans arrived en masse to pay their respects to their tragically departed player with more than 29,000 attending the match, which was won 6-2 by a Scotland XI. White's brother Tommy appeared as a 'guest' for Spurs in the game. The result was insignificant, but did allow Spurs fans a first glimpse of Alan Gilzean who signed from Dundee soon after.

SATURDAY 12th NOVEMBER 1960

Second meet first when Spurs travel to Hillsborough with Sheffield Wednesday coming out on top. It is Spurs' first defeat of the season as they go down 2-1 in South Yorkshire. Spurs can take pride in the fact it took them 17 matches to finish a game with nothing to show for their efforts as Maurice Norman's goal is not enough to keep the run going.

SUNDAY 12th NOVEMBER 2006

Robbie Keane's 24th-minute penalty puts Tottenham 1-0 up at Reading, but the Royals bounce back to win 3-1 on a forgettable day for Martin Jol's men. Nicky Shorey and Dave Kitson make it 2-1 before the break and Kevin Doyle seals the hosts' victory ten minutes from time.

SATURDAY 13th NOVEMBER 1920

Spurs score ten goals in eight days against Oldham Athletic, including this 5-2 victory at Boundary Park. The goals in the north-west come from Jimmy Seed and Charlie Wilson, who both net twice. Bert Bliss completes the scoring on the day as Spurs dominate the fixture in a season where they manage to finish sixth.

STEFFEN IVERSEN HELPS SPURS RECORD AN IMPRESSIVE 3-1 WIN AT LIVERPOOL IN NOVEMBER 1998.

SATURDAY 13th NOVEMBER 2004

Spurs score four times against Arsenal but still lose at White Hart Lane in an amazing north London derby. Noureddine Naybet puts the Lilywhites ahead on 37 minutes but Thierry Henry and Lauren fire the Gunners 2-1 up with 55 minutes gone. Patrick Vieira makes it 3-1 on the hour before Jermain Defoe scores 60 seconds later. Freddie Ljungberg then makes it 4-2 on 69 minutes. Ledley King pulls another back on 74 but Robert Pires adds a fifth ten minutes from time. There is still time for Freddie Kanoute to make it 4-5 to complete a breathless encounter.

SATURDAY 14th NOVEMBER 1998

George Graham takes his Tottenham team to Highbury for the first time since his return to north London. He was only five games into his reign, but he had already made his mark on the team, by creating a very defensively-minded formation which Spurs fans took an instant dislike to. Although the Lilywhites manage to restrict Arsenal's probing in the 0-0 draw, the Man of the Match award was still given to Spurs goalkeeper, Espen Baardsen. Many Tottenham fans leave wondering whether they really want a team who can grind out results or a return to the free-flowing football the team have traditionally always tried to play. Easy answer!

TUESDAY 15th NOVEMBER 1994

Gerry Francis is appointed as the club's new manager. The new arrival had quit Queens Park Rangers after they attempted to bring in Rodney Marsh as their chief executive. He was the club's third manager in two years, enjoying a three-year stay in charge at White Hart Lane, without any notable successes.

SATURDAY 16th NOVEMBER 1991

Four second-half goals gives Spurs a comfortable win over Luton Town at White Hart Lane. The hosts are behind when the floodlights fail, causing a 15-minute delay, but it's Spurs who return with batteries recharged to dominate the match when play resumes. Spurs score four times in the final quarter of the match, with substitute Scott Houghton and Gary Lineker both netting twice on an illuminating evening in north London.

SATURDAY 17th NOVEMBER 2001

Glenn Hoddle's first home game in charge couldn't have been much tougher with the visitors being a strong Arsenal side. Both teams score once each in a game which also sees Sol Campbell return to White Hart Lane for the first time since his departure to Highbury. The home fans made their feelings towards Campbell clear, but it was Arsenal who tapped into the fiery atmosphere by taking the lead in the second period. Gus Poyet equalises with a volley to guarantee a point for Hoddle's men as Campbell leaves the pitch with his ears ringing.

SATURDAY 18th NOVEMBER 1950

Spurs demolish Newcastle United at White Hart Lane, scoring seven times without reply. Arthur Rowe's side were purveying a style of football which was taking the league by storm and this performance was one of the best examples of its merits. Les Bennett, Eddie Baily and Les Medley set Tottenham on their way with three early goals in front of over 70,000 fans. Medley went on to net a hat-trick with Sonny Walters and Alf Ramsey adding their names to the score-sheet.

SATURDAY 19th NOVEMBER 1887

Tottenham Marshes play host to the first fixture between Spurs and Arsenal. Admittedly, at the time, the opposition were named Woolwich Arsenal and based in the south of London. It was a mildly farcical event with Arsenal arriving late for the match which had to be abandoned due to bad light. When the game was called off with 15 minutes remaining, Spurs were leading 2-1. Bragging rights, anyone?

WEDNESDAY 20th NOVEMBER 1968

Spurs travel to Highbury to play Arsenal in a cup competition for only the second time in the two clubs' history. The occasion was the first leg of the League Cup semi-final and it was the home side who gained the advantage late on, when a poor Joe Kinnear header was intercepted and punished to give Arsenal a 1-0 first-leg lead.

SATURDAY 20th NOVEMBER 2010

Arsenal go 2-0 up at half-time thanks to goals from Samir Nasri and Marouane Chamakh and Spurs' appalling record at the old foes looks like stretching to 70 games. Harry Redknapp delivers an inspirational team-talk at the break and Gareth Bale makes it 2-1 within five minutes of the re-start. Rafael van der Vaart then makes it 2-2 from the penalty spot before Younes Kaboul grabs a winner on 85 minutes that sends 3,000 Spurs fans into ecstasy and gives the Lilywhites a first win away to the Gunners for 17 years.

SATURDAY 21st NOVEMBER 1931

Spurs score nine goals in a match for the first time in their history with Port Vale the unfortunate victims in a one-sided Second Division clash. George Hunt lays the platform for the win with a brace, with winger Willie Davies getting a hat-trick. The other goals come from Jimmy Brain, who notches a double, whilst Dave Colquhoun and Albert Lyons score once each in the 9-3 win.

SATURDAY 22nd NOVEMBER 1986

Clive Allen's 13th and 14th goals of the season put Spurs in command as they defeat Oxford 4-2 at the Manor Ground. The U's were undefeated at home and take the lead, but Spurs' bounce back when Allen nets twice in quick succession to give his team the lead. Chris Waddle then matches Allen's feat with two of his own to seal a 4-2 victory.

SUNDAY 22nd NOVEMBER 2009

Records tumble as Spurs humiliate Wigan in a 9-1 massacre at White Hart Lane. Incredibly, only Peter Crouch's goal separates the teams at the break before Jermain Defoe gets the first of five goals on 51 minutes and adds his second three minutes later. Paul Scharner then makes it 3-1 before Defoe resumes the mantle, completing his hat-trick just before the hour. His seven-minute treble is the second fastest in Premier League history. Aaron Lennon makes it 5-1 shortly after and Defoe gets his fourth on 69 minutes. His fifth against the punch-drunk Latics comes on 87 minutes and there is still time for David Bentley and Niko Kranjcar to add two more to complete Tottenham's biggest top-flight win.

YOUNES KABOUL HEADS A FAMOUS LAST-MINUTE WINNER AT ARSENAL IN NOVEMBER 2010.

WEDNESDAY 23rd NOVEMBER 1983

Spurs travel to Munich for a Uefa Cup tie hoping to avenge their loss against the Germans the previous season. It was -5°C on the night, making conditions tricky for both sides, and a hard-fought game was won in the final few minutes with Bayern snatching a late winner to give them a slight advantage for the return leg in England.

MONDAY 24th NOVEMBER 1975

Spurs net two goals in extra time to overcome a stubborn West Ham United in a League Cup fourth-round replay. After 180 goalless minutes, Spurs finally break the deadlock as Scottish centre-half Willie Young scores the opener before John Duncan calms the nerves with a second to guarantee the team's progression to the next round.

SATURDAY 25th NOVEMBER 2000

A Les Ferdinand hat-trick was enough to see off Leicester City at White Hart Lane. The visitors from the East Midlands had no response to the striker's unstoppable form on the day to give George Graham's side their seventh home victory in their opening eight games of the season in north London, as Spurs fans start to warm to the former Arsenal boss.

SATURDAY 26th NOVEMBER 1977

Spurs travel to the north-west to face Bolton Wanderers in a top-of-the-table clash at Burnden Park and lose to a late goal. Tottenham were arguably the better team for long periods but looked to be heading for at least a point when the hosts grab an 89th-minute winner to send the Trotters four points clear of the Lilywhites at the top.

SATURDAY 26th NOVEMBER 2005

Martin Jol celebrates his 50th game in charge of Spurs with a 2-1 win away to third place Wigan Athletic. Robbie Keane (eight minutes) and a 77th-minute goal from Edgar Davids is enough to render Lee McCulloch's late goal no more than a consolation. The win lifts Spurs to fifth, level on points with Manchester United.

WEDNESDAY 27th NOVEMBER 1996

Spurs are humiliated by First Division Bolton Wanderers in the League Cup fourth round, when Wanderers beat them 6-1 at Burnden Park. The hosts take the lead, but are pegged back by Teddy Sheringham. Bolton regain the lead to go into the break with a 2-1 lead and then net four more times before the final whistle blows. Not a memorable night, especially for the couple of thousand travelling fans.

WEDNESDAY 28th NOVEMBER 1984

Spurs get through a nervy first leg against Bohemians Prague at White Hart Lane with a two-goal lead. The hosts were fortunate to get the goals they did, with the first coming from a Prague defender diverting the ball into his own net. The visitors then dominated the game, and were unlucky not to grab an equaliser, which made it all the more painful for them when Gary Stevens added a second for Spurs against the run of play.

SUNDAY 28th NOVEMBER 2010

Martin Skrtel scores at both ends and Aaron Lennon grabs a dramatic injury-time winner as Spurs beat Liverpool 2-1 at White Hart Lane. Skrtel opens the scoring by finding the net on 42 minutes and Liverpool miss a great chance to double the lead minutes later. Just past the hour, Jermain Defoe blazed a penalty wide before Skrtel put through his own goal four minutes later. With a point likely for both teams, Lennon prods Peter Crouch's pass home to send the home fans wild.

SATURDAY 29th NOVEMBER 1997

Christian Gross' first game in charge goes swimmingly for the Swiss manager, as Spurs comfortably ease past Everton 2-0 at Goodison Park. It was Gross' compatriot Ramon Vega that put Spurs into the lead with the charismatic David Ginola putting the game out of reach of the Toffees. Espen Baardsen put in a fantastic display in goal for Spurs, which earned the Norwegian the Man of the Match honours. Arguably, this would be one of the highs of Gross' troubled spell at White Hart Lane.

THURSDAY 29th NOVEMBER 2007

Danish side AAB Aalborg take a shock 2-0 lead in the Uefa Cup at White Hart Lane but Spurs roar back in the second half to win this five-goal thriller. The visitors find themselves two goals to the good after just 27 minutes but Dimitar Berbatov and Steed Malbranque make it 2-2 within six minutes of the re-start before Darren Bent secures victory on 66 minutes.

SATURDAY 30th NOVEMBER 1957

Spurs claim their first away win of the season at the usually unlucky destination of Old Trafford. It's quite a feat, considering that Manchester United were third in the league at the time and the home side also took the lead, but Spurs soon came into their own, scoring four times in 25 frantic minutes. Bobby Smith scores twice, before Danny Blanchflower's brother, Jackie, scored an own goal to give Spurs a third and Smith soon added a fourth to complete his hat-trick. United pull two goals back to make it a tense finish, but Spurs manage to hold on to give them the points and a rare success in the red half of Manchester.

SATURDAY 30th NOVEMBER 2002

Birmingham City prove a tough nut to crack at St Andrew's in front of a partisan crowd of almost 30,000. It's the travelling fans who celebrate the first goal, however, with Teddy Sheringham scoring in the 55th minute. Jeff Kenna levels for Blues on 68 minutes to earn a share of the spoils.

SUNDAY 30th NOVEMBER 2008

Harry Redknapp, who has steered Spurs away from the foot of the Premier League with seven wins in his first nine games in charge, sees Everton leave White Hart Lane with a 1-0 win – their fifth on the road in eight matches. Ironically, the winner is scored by a Spurs player, with Vedran Corluka credited with an own goal on 51 minutes in David Moyes' 300th game in charge of the Toffees. It leaves Tottenham still perilously close to the drop zone while the visitors go seventh.

SPURS
On This Day

DECEMBER

SATURDAY 1st DECEMBER 1990

An unfortunate sequence of events leads to farce as the Tottenham team coach is towed away from outside a London hotel while the team have lunch prior to playing Chelsea. The coach includes the team's kit and the late arrival at Stamford Bridge results in a fine from the FA. An omen for the match ahead, perhaps, Paul Gascoigne and Gary Lineker score for Spurs but Chelsea still triumph 3-2.

WEDNESDAY 2nd DECEMBER 1998

Spurs advance to the League Cup semi-final after defeating a weakened Manchester United team 3-1. Chris Armstrong shows his prowess in the air by scoring two headers in quick succession to set Spurs on their way. The win was completed by a fantastic David Ginola strike from distance that nestled in the top corner, much to the delight of the White Hart Lane faithful.

TUESDAY 3rd DECEMBER 1963

Spurs despatch Manchester United at White Hart Lane in the first leg of the European Cup Winners' Cup. Goals from Dave Mackay on the hour, and Bobby Smith in the 87th minute, make the difference against United as Spurs take a crucial two-goal advantage going into the second game at Old Trafford.

SATURDAY 4th DECEMBER 1965

Frank Saul is the first Tottenham player to be sent off in a league game in 37 years when he is dismissed against Burnley at Turf Moor. The match finishes 1-1, with Eddie Clayton netting Spurs' only goal of a game played in front of 19,500 spectators on a chilly Lancashire afternoon.

SATURDAY 5th DECEMBER 1998

Spurs beat Liverpool 2-1 at White Hart Lane thanks to Ruel Fox's first-half strike, and an own goal from the unfortunate Jamie Carragher. The home team dominate the majority of the game and should have converted more of the chances created. Both goals came from good wing play, with the classy Frenchman David Ginola – surely born to be a Tottenham player – using his skill down the left to great effect and ultimately proving the difference between two well-matched teams.

WEDNESDAY 6th DECEMBER 1972

Spurs dump Liverpool out of the League Cup in a replay at White Hart Lane just two days after drawing at Anfield in the league. The Lilywhites take a two-goal lead early on as John Pratt and Martin Chivers give the hosts breathing space in the opening 15 minutes. Chivers went on to add a second to seal an impressive 3-1 win over Bill Shankly's men, and earn a semi-final place to boot.

WEDNESDAY 7th DECEMBER 1983

A 2-0 win avenges the previous season's loss to Bayern Munich in the European Cup Winners' Cup. Spurs were one goal behind from the first leg in Germany, but come out of the blocks all guns blazing to overturn the deficit. A Steve Archibald strike levels the tie and Spurs deservedly score a second with only four minutes left on the clock, as Glenn Hoddle sends Mark Falco free on goal to finish with aplomb. The closing moments prove frantic as Spurs desperately try to keep out the Bundesliga outfit but with fingernails bitten to the limit, the referee ends the torture and Spurs march on.

TUESDAY 8th DECEMBER 1971

Spurs beat Rapid Bucharest 3-0 at White Lane Hart in a Uefa Cup third-round tie. Martin Peters gets the Lilywhites off to a flier by scoring after only 20 seconds of the game and Chivers holds off two defenders to calmly finish and double the lead on 37 minutes. The Romanians, believing their goalkeeper had been impeded, begin to protest on the pitch with the Bucharest custodian threatening to walk off. The game eventually restarts with Chivers adding a third after 67 minutes.

MONDAY 8th DECEMBER 2008

Ledley Kings marks his 250th game for Tottenham with a 68th-minute goal to open Tottenham's account at West Ham United. King's effort, followed by a period of intense pressure by the Hammers, is enough for the three points at Upton Park, but Jamie O'Hara makes sure with a second on 90 minutes to make it a happy journey back from east London for 3,000 or so Spurs supporters.

SATURDAY 9th DECEMBER 1967

Most of Britain wakes to find a blanket of snow and with Manchester City due to take on Tottenham at Maine Road, most supporters assume the game will be called off. However, with the Mancunians building up a head of steam in the league, the fans and players were desperate for the match to go ahead – and the referee passes the pitch fit to play. City boss Joe Mercer decides to let his players warm up an hour before kick-off – and it proved to be one of his many managerial masterstrokes with Spurs opting to warm up inside. Tony Book suggested his team-mates unscrew their studs to expose a small screw – just enough for grip in the treacherous conditions – and City come out and play with sure-footed grace that had Spurs on the rack virtually from the word go. Jimmy Greaves still manages to put Spurs ahead before the snow began to fall again. City storm back in almost blizzard-like conditions to score goals through Colin Bell, Mike Summerbee, Tony Coleman and Neil Young. Legendary Everton striker Dixie Dean describes City's display as one of the best he has ever seen and the press were so taken by City's performance that it became known as 'The Ballet on Ice'. Spurs travel home well beaten, but having played their part in an excellent game of football.

FRIDAY 9th DECEMBER 1994

Spurs are reinstated to the FA Cup thanks to a passionate plea from chairman Alan Sugar in front of a Football Association panel. The Lilywhites had been banned from the competition for a year due to indiscretions made by the previous board which Sugar saw as incredibly unfair and vowed to get the decision changed. On this day, he proved he was as good as his word.

THURSDAY 10th DECEMBER 1931

Peter Baker is born in Hampstead. The full-back played almost 300 league games for Spurs from 1952 to 1965 and was part of the 1961 double-winning side. He left the club at the age of 33 to move to South African side Durban United, where he played for a season, before becoming the club's manager. Baker stayed in the country after retiring, turning over a new leaf by running a stationery company.

TUESDAY 10th DECEMBER 1963

Manchester United get the better of Spurs in a 4-1 win, sending the club crashing out of the European Cup Winners' Cup on a costly night for the Lilywhites. The start was ominous as United take the lead after only six minutes, and then skipper Dave Mackay was stretchered off with a broken leg only moments later. This was in the days before substitutes meaning Spurs had to play on with only ten men for the next 83 minutes. The effort level was too great, with United adding a second just after the interval. Jimmy Greaves pulls one back, but United were in the ascendency, and add two more before the final whistle blows.

TUESDAY 11th DECEMBER 1962

Spurs defeat Rangers 3-2 in the European Cup Winners' Cup at Ibrox, sending them through to the next round. Tottenham were already three goals ahead from the first leg, with Jimmy Greaves extending the aggregate lead after eight minutes to silence the 80,000 fans in the stadium. Rangers equalised in the second half, but normal service was resumed when Bobby Smith nets for Spurs. The Scots would not lie down, equalising once more, before Les Allen scored the winner late on.

WEDNESDAY 12th DECEMBER 1973

Dinamo Tbilisi are destroyed at White Hart Lane, as Spurs smash five goals past the Georgians. Chris McGrath starts the rout in the first half, with the other strikes coming in the second period. A Ralph Coates cross is converted by Martin Chivers before Tbilisi pull one back to mean another goal would put them through, but Spurs shift through the gears and go on to dominate the final quarter with Martin Peters scoring twice more and Chivers adding another.

MONDAY 12th DECEMBER 2005

A sizzling second-half display sees Spurs recover from 1-0 down to Portsmouth to win 3-1. Lomana Lua Lua's spectacular 25-yard goal gives Pompey a 24th-minute lead that they hang on to until half-time, but it's a different home side that emerge from the White Hart Lane tunnel after the break with Ledley King levelling before Mido and Jermain Defoe both score in the closing minutes to secure a 3-1 win.

WEDNESDAY 13th DECEMBER 1967

A 4-3 win isn't enough for Spurs, as Olympique Lyonnais advance to the next round of the European Cup Winners' Cup on the away goals rule. Spurs were lacking defenders due to injuries and it was mistakes at the back that would be the team's downfall. In a topsy-turvy game, goals from Martin Chivers, Cliff Jones and Alan Gilzean give hope, but the first-leg deficit can only be matched and the French side's goal haul at the Lane sees them progress.

SATURDAY 14th DECEMBER 1912

Everything pointed to a Spurs loss on a manic day as they attempted to get to Woolwich to face Arsenal. The team bus was delayed, and then stopped by police as they attempted to make up time. Spurs arrived at Manor Field just before kick-off, but had few worries as they defeated Arsenal in the last meeting between the two before the team moved to north London and became genuine rivals. Bobby Steel opened the scoring with the great Jimmy Cantrell netting twice to give Spurs a 3-0 win.

WEDNESDAY 14th DECEMBER 1960

Chris Waddle is born in Felling. The talented winger struggled to find a professional club as a youngster, and started off at non-league Tow Law Town while supplementing his income by working in a sausage factory. He is eventually snapped up by Newcastle for £1,000. Waddle proves a huge hit for the north-east outfit, where he eventually catches the attention of Spurs, who sign him in 1985. He goes on to make 138 league appearances for the Lilywhites. Waddle moved to Marseille in 1989 for £4.5m.

WEDNESDAY 15th DECEMBER 1971

Spurs brush Rapid Bucharest aside with a 2-0 win in Romania to guarantee a place in the hat for the fourth round of the Uefa Cup. Tensions are high when Jimmy Pearce scores the opening goal with the Romanians claiming he was offside which creates an extended argument with the officials and Spurs players. Moments later, Pearce is dismissed along with a Rapid defender following an on-pitch 'disagreement'. Martin Chivers completes the scoring when he nets a decisive second with a few minutes to play.

SATURDAY 16th DECEMBER 1961

Jimmy Greaves shows exactly what Tottenham have bought when he starts his Spurs career and scores a hat-trick on his debut against Blackpool following his return to England. The Lilywhites pay £99,999 to bring the former Chelsea striker back from AC Milan and the decision to smash the club's transfer fee is justified immediately. Spurs defeat the Tangerines 5-2 and Greaves' treble includes a spectacular bicycle kick. Les Allen was the other Spurs player to get on the score-sheet, as he bags a double, rising to the challenge set by his new team-mate.

MONDAY 16th DECEMBER 1991

Two years after scoring the championship-winning goal for Arsenal at Anfield, England international Michael Thomas completes a move to Liverpool and makes his debut in a 2-1 victory over Spurs at White Hart Lane. The Spurs faithful 'welcome' Thomas with sustained jeering throughout, but it fails to knock Thomas off his stride and he plays an important part in the Reds' victory.

SATURDAY 17th DECEMBER 1960

Spurs stay top of the league by defeating Everton at Goodison Park. On a foggy day in Liverpool, it is the visitors who dominate the match with Johnny White opening Tottenham's account. Les Allen doubles the lead a few minutes later. Everton reduce the deficit, but Dave Mackay restores the two-goal advantage on the hour mark, putting the game out of reach of the home side and sealing a 3-1 win.

SATURDAY 18th DECEMBER 1993

Six goals are shared with Liverpool at White Hart Lane as Spurs fight back from being 3-1 down against the Reds. Vinny Samways gets his first of the season to give the home side the lead going into half-time. However, within nine minutes of the re-start, Liverpool had scored three times forcing Spurs to attack in order to salvage something from the game. Micky Hazard and Darren Caskey manage to do just that as Spurs rally to take a point from a pulsating game.

SATURDAY 19th DECEMBER 1959

Spurs see off Newcastle United at White Hart Lane, scoring four goals without reply to go top of the league. Both sides struggled to get to grips with a waterlogged pitch, but it's Spurs who prevail with Maurice Norman heading home the opener. Cliff Jones soon adds a second to give Tottenham a two-goal cushion heading into the interval. After the break, Johnny White and Danny Blanchflower each net a goal to guarantee the points and put Bill Nicholson's team top of the table following Preston North End's remarkable 5-4 home defeat to Chelsea.

WEDNESDAY 20th DECEMBER 1972

Spurs gain the upper hand from the first leg of their League Cup semi-final against Wolverhampton Wanderers at Molineux. Two goals in 15 minutes set Spurs on their way, as Martin Peters and John Pratt get their names on the score-sheet. Wolves gave themselves a chance heading into the second leg, when they scored a penalty in the second period.

SATURDAY 21st DECEMBER 1957

A Bobby Smith brace plays an important part in Spurs' 4-2 win at Stamford Bridge. The other scorers for the Lilywhites are Terry Medwin and Tommy Harmer. The win enables Tottenham to clamber over their London rivals into ninth spot in Division One.

SATURDAY 21st DECEMBER 2001

Ipswich Town come from 1-0 down to beat Spurs 2-1 at White Hart Lane. Simon Davies gives the hosts the lead but Finidi George and Alun Armstrong give George Burley's men all three points.

SATURDAY 22nd DECEMBER 1990

Nine-man Spurs come from behind to win at home against Luton Town. Nayim and Pat van den Hauwe had both seen red; the former for foul and abusive language, and the Belgian for a poor tackle. With Spurs looking to contain the visitors and already a goal down, striker Paul Stewart was forced to play in midfield for the remainder of the game. However, it proves to be an inspired move as the out-of-form forward scores twice to give Tottenham an unlikely victory.

SATURDAY 22nd DECEMBER 2007

Robbie Keane misses a penalty and Spurs concede a late goal to lose 2-1 in a miserable north London derby. Emmanuel Adebayor had given the Gunners the lead at the Emirates but Dimitar Berbatov levels on 66 minutes, five minutes before Keane misses his spot kick. Nicklas Bendtner hits the winner ten minutes from time.

WEDNESDAY 23rd DECEMBER 1970

Spurs confirm their passage to the League Cup Final by defeating Bristol City in the second leg of the semi at White Hart Lane. Two goals are enough to see Spurs through to Wembley, after a score draw at Ashton Gate. The 90 minutes pass without incident and it would take extra time for the victors to emerge. Martin Chivers and Jimmy Pearce prove to be the difference as they score the decisive goals late on to send the Robins crashing out.

MONDAY 23rd DECEMBER 2002

Ten-man Spurs hang on to victory at Manchester City in an incident packed 3-2 win. Steve Howey gives the Blues the lead, but Chris Perry, Simon Davies and Gus Poyet reply for Glenn Hoddle's side who also see Christian Ziege sent off. Ali Benarbia scores in injury time but it's too little, too late.

SATURDAY 24th DECEMBER 1932

Despite Spurs easily being the highest scorers in Division Two, the Lilywhites only manage one goal in the 2-1 defeat to Notts County on Christmas Eve 1932. It's a blow to Tottenham's title hopes and it sees the club drop down to fourth spot, five points behind leaders Stoke City.

SUNDAY 24th DECEMBER 1955

Scoring sensation Bobby Smith makes his debut against Luton Town at White Hart Lane, though the striker doesn't have much of an impact on this occasion. It is Johnny Brooks and Len Duquemin who score the goals on a day when the quality of football is hampered by a muddy pitch. Not that too many complaints were registered as Spurs win 2-1 and bank two very valuable points in their bid to move away from the foot of the table.

GUS POYET CELEBRATES HIS GOAL AT MANCHESTER CITY IN DECEMBER 2002.

THURSDAY 25th DECEMBER 1952

Spurs provide a festive feast to score seven against Middlesbrough at home. The Christmas Day game was a tradition up until 1958, with this being one of the more memorable games played that day. Les Bennett scored a cracker after 12 minutes, but Boro found parity soon afterwards. In the second half a partially injured Bennett nets three more times, with Len Duquemin adding a brace and Eddie Baily getting one to add a little more joy to the festive season for the Tottenham faithful.

THURSDAY 25th DECEMBER 1958

Tottenham's star continues to fade as they slip to just one point off the bottom of Division One with a galling 2-1 defeat away to West Ham United. The Lilywhites' all-too real relegation fears make it a miserable Christmas Day for Spurs' travelling support, but at least it's the last time matches will be played on this particular date as sense prevails at FA HQ and Christmas Days become the one day of the year players will no longer play competitive matches.

SATURDAY 26th DECEMBER 1964

Spurs earn maximum points away from home for the first time in 11 attempts, as they beat Nottingham Forest at the City Ground on Boxing Day. Alan Gilzean scores the first for Spurs in only his second game for the club to invigorate the side. The winner was netted by Welsh winger Cliff Jones, as Spurs end their away-day hoodoo with a welcome win in the East Midlands. If only the Lilywhites could repeat some of their home form where they had won ten of the dozen games played to that point.

SUNDAY 26th DECEMBER 2010

Rafael van der Vaart scores twice as Spurs enjoy a Boxing Day win at Aston Villa. The Dutch midfielder scores on 23 and 67 minutes to render Marc Albrighton's late goal no more than a consolatory effort for the struggling Midlands outfit. Almost 40,000 attend a game that sees fifth-place Spurs close the gap on Chelsea in fourth to one point.

SATURDAY 27th DECEMBER 1952

Spurs make it 11 goals in two games as they thrash Middlesbrough for the second time in three days. It was the perfect Christmas present for Spurs considering that sandwiched between two great wins was a long journey up to the north-east. On the day, Spurs hit four unanswered goals with Sonny Walters, Len Duquemin and Les Bennett getting one each, with the Teessiders' painful experience compounded by an own goal.

SUNDAY 28th DECEMBER 1997

A north London derby ends in a 1-1 draw thanks to the intervention of Spurs' Danish star Allan Nielsen, who scores Spurs' goal on the half hour. It is a well-deserved point after some poor results in the previous weeks, but despite being the better team for large passages of play, the Gunners net an equaliser on the hour mark.

SATURDAY 29th DECEMBER 1984

Spurs make it nine games unbeaten as Sunderland are sent packing from White Hart Lane with nothing to show for their efforts. The hosts are too strong for the relegation-threatened Mackems and quality finishes from Glenn Hoddle and Garth Crooks settle the game.

SATURDAY 30th DECEMBER 1972

Tottenham book their place in the 1972/73 League Cup Final as they draw at home with Wolverhampton Wanderers in the second leg of their semi-final. Spurs had a 2-1 advantage from the first leg, which is quickly lost as Terry Naylor puts the ball into this own net. Martin Peters pounces to level the game on the night but Wolves score late on to force extra time. Eventually, Martin Chivers grabs what proves to be the overall winner to put Spurs through to Wembley after making it 2-2 on the night.

SATURDAY 30th DECEMBER 2000

Spurs' miserable away form continues with a 3-0 defeat at Ipswich Town. It means the Lilywhites have taken just two points out of a possible 33 on the road while the Tractor Boys move up to third in the Premier League.

SUNDAY 30th DECEMBER 2006

Liverpool end Tottenham's run of 12 successive home wins in all competitions with a barely deserved 1-0 win at White Hart Lane. The Reds' goal comes on half-time when Spanish midfielder Luis Garcia scores the only goal of the game to spoil the Lilywhites' proud home record, but boss Martin Jol blames the absence of Jermaine Jenas, Robbie Keane and Aaron Lennon – plus a poorly Dimitar Berbatov – who climbs off his sickbed to come on as a substitute, ultimately in vain.

SATURDAY 31st DECEMBER 1921

Spurs warm up for their New Year's celebrations by hammering Preston North End 5-0 at White Hart Lane. The Lancastrians never get a foothold in the game as Spurs dominate from start to finish. Charlie Wilson does the most damage by scoring twice, but he is ably assisted by Jimmy Seed, Andy Thompson and Jimmy Dimmock who each net once. The win moves the Lilywhites up several places in the league table – and above Preston.

SATURDAY 31st DECEMBER 1938

Spurs endure a nightmarish end to the year when they crash 4-0 at Coventry City. The Lilywhites, unbeaten at home in a dozen games, miss the chance to go into the top six with an awful performance at Highfield Road.

SATURDAY 31st DECEMBER 2005

Traditionally, this is a date Spurs do very well on and it's a run that continues with a ninth win in ten previous games on December 31st. Goals from Teemu Tainio and Mido are enough to beat Newcastle United and keep Martin Jol's side hot on the trail of third-place Liverpool as the race for Champions League football ratchets up a notch. The last day of the year has, traditionally, been particularly fruitful for the Lilywhites who have won ten of the 14 games played on this date, scoring 37 goals and conceding just 16.

TEEMU TAINIO AND MIDO CELEBRATE DURING THE 2-0 WIN OVER NEWCASTLE UNITED IN DECEMBER 2005.